BARE: 10 Houses To 10 Bags

"BARE - MY JOURNEY FROM OWNING 10 HOUSES TO BEING HOMELESS WITH 10 BAGS"

By Jonquil G

ISBN 13: 978-0-9601321-0-2

I dedicate this book to you, my three sons, Brandon, Ryan, and Jonathan. I love you with all my heart. Thank you for your encouragement and excitement as we dreamed together. I am so grateful for your support and patience during this process. The three of you gave me the courage to do better and be better with each passing day as I continued to write about our journey and the journeys of some of the families who have crossed our paths year after year. I wrote this book in hopes of healing the four of us and others. Thank you for loving and believing in me and for helping me to believe in myself during the difficult times. Thank you for being willing to make the many sacrifices you endured during the hard years and for remaining faithful despite how things looked as we dreamed together. I have been blessed with you, my three brilliant and gifted sons, who are wise beyond your years. I have learned so much from all of you. I pray you will live lives beyond your wildest dreams. This book was completed because you believed I could and would do it. I love you all forever and always, no matter what!

Truly Yours,

Mom

To Pastor Rock, with much love and gratitude. You will be remembered as a huge blessing to me and my sons. You showed us the meaning of truly being a pastor with a beautiful servant's heart. You always knew what we needed and when we needed it without my having to ask. I am so grateful to you for your hours of counseling, encouragement, and support. I so appreciated you reading the first half of my book, then preaching from it to let me know that you liked my message and to encourage me to continue writing during a season that was quite difficult. It was not only up-lifting, but it was also a surprise and blessing to hear my message and to see the reaction of others to it that Sunday. You were an amazing friend, and I am so thankful that you were so in-tune and obedient to call me whenever God prompted you that I was in distress. You were a gifted counselor and were so patient as I sat in your office and cried rivers of cleansing tears before we talked, finding the root of my issue. I would not be who I am today if it were not for all that you did as you shepherded us over the years before you went to your heavenly home.

To Pastors Natalie and Robert Greene, Kingdom Fountain of Life Ministry. I am so very grateful to you both for the lovingkindness you have shown to me as our paths crossed over the past decade plus. I am very grateful for your spiritual counsel, mentoring and training in seasons of my life. You are both wonderful Shepherds and I am very grateful God placed you in my life.

To my family, thank you for loving me. I am very grateful and blessed that God gave each of you to me. I have learned much from each of you that has helped to mold me into who I am today. I love all of you.

To all the many friends and associates, there are too many of you to mention individually so I sincerely thank you for all the many lessons learned from each of you. I am so appreciative for all of you as divine connections in various seasons of my life and I am blessed to have crossed paths with you.

To the many Titus Women, the mentors who came along side me over the years teaching, leading, and praying with me, I sincerely thank you all for all you have done to bless me.

To my readers and editors, Mozella Bourda, Pastor Rock, Joyce Ward, Hanne Moon, and Shelese Douglas, thank you for suggestions, reading and edits to the first few editions your help was invaluable for this book to give voice to my story and the opportunity to lend my voice to those unable to share their stories themselves for various reasons. I am so incredibly grateful to you and your keen eyes and wonderful suggestions.

To Sandi Coughlin, a very special thank you for capturing the image that I saw in a vision that God gave me for my book cover for this Bare series. You are truly a gifted photographer, and I am forever grateful for our divine connection.

To the many pastors, prayer warriors and prophets that God sent to me over the years to give me various messages, I sincerely thank you for being obedient in delivering the messages. These messages and prayers greatly blessed me, especially during times of struggles and confusion.

To Paula Giesey, thank you for consistently calling to pray with me weekly and for interceding on my behalf. I am so very grateful for your listening ears and wise counsel that has helped me more than words could express.

To Natalie Brown, thank you for helping me by answering questions with Word and creating spreadsheets and documents as well as teaching me how to use some tools. I appreciate you being one of my readers, editors and for your typesetting expertise to make this book visually appealing. I am so grateful for your constant encouragement and support through this arduous process of publishing. I am grateful for you.

To Julie Erickson, I am so grateful for our divine connection because you were an answered prayer when you arrived at the homeless shelter to teach Oola Classes. Those classes encouraged me to dream again and to set new goals for my new life in that season. I am also grateful for your Rolling Classes that relieved the huge amount of stress stored in my body that I was dealing with due to having so many roommates while at the shelter as well as dealing the hostile work environment at the job that I had at the time. This book would not have been completed without your assistance in editing and your final reading after edits were made. I am so grateful for your kindness and encouragement. I love your wellness journal "Season of Growth", it has been very helpful. www.massageetcllc.com

To Renee Davidson, Made 2 Roar Ministry. I am so very grateful for you and your kindness shown to me with the Freedom Prayer Sessions that I have had with you on a weekly basis that helped me come out of hiding to be able to courageously stand to be heard and seen in the completion of this book. I am so grateful to God for bringing you into my life to help me become equipped and prepared for my new life as I transformed emotionally, mentally, spiritually and physically. www.made2roar.org

To my friend since childhood Sandra Miller, I am so grateful that you found me online and reconnected to me in 2008. You are answered prayers. I so appreciate you sending your book to me as a gift during my divorce when I needed your book most *"Balancing Blessings and Obtaining Order: 11 Steps to Balancing your Life, Organizing your Possessions, and Walking in the Spirit of God"* it helped me greatly when my life was flipped upside down and inside out. You have walked through this book with me over the years giving me advice as my book developed and unfolded along my journey. Thank you for creating my banner for my social media and for creating the book cover. I so appreciate your assistance, loyalty and continued encouragement even during my toughest times of heaviness and despair you remained positive, supportive, and a tried-and-true intercessor and destiny helper, always praying and speaking only what and how God instructed you to speak that would best help me continue moving forward with hope. I am so grateful for all you have done and your tender giving heart, you blessed me beyond what words could express. www.balancingblessingsbk.com

Dear Reader,

The stories in this book are based on my healing journey and that of others walking with me. If names are used, the names have been changed to protect the privacy of those I have had the privilege to see healed. It is my hope and prayer that you will be encouraged to heal and transform yourself as well. I must tell you; I do not have any title with -ian or -ist in it. That being stated, know that I am not, nor do I claim to be, a physician, clinician, psychologist, therapist, strategist, or lawyer. I am a fifty-seven-year-old mother of three sons and a student of life who hopes to inspire others to transform emotionally, mentally, physically, spiritually, and financially to live a life beyond their wildest dreams. The information I share within these pages is intended to encourage only; it should not be construed as professional advice. Seek knowledge, advice, and services from specific industry professionals. We are blessed with the ability to fulfill our hearts' desires in life, and it is my hope that you will give yourself permission to focus on your needs and dreams. I am not responsible for anything good or bad that happens in your life—taking responsibility for your life is how you take the first step in this journey of new beginnings. We must trust God to take what was meant for harm and use it for our benefit and the benefit of others. As I stated previously, I am simply a woman who has picked up some information while on my journey. This information is not intended to be, nor should it be construed to be, professional medical, psychological, financial, or legal advice. The whole premise of this book is to encourage you to ask the right questions, seek useful knowledge, and knock on the doors that would open to opportunities for a healthy, balanced, and prosperous life.

Dare to be "Bare" and live a life beyond your wildest
dreams,

Jonquil

N OTHING IN ALL CREATION IS
HIDDEN FROM GOD'S SIGHT.
EVERYTHING IS UNCOVERED AND LAID
BARE BEFORE THE EYES OF HIM TO
WHOM WE MUST GIVE ACCOUNT.

Hebrews 4:13 NIV

Table of Contents

~ *Introduction* ~

I have a secret to tell you! Well, I actually need to confess several secrets. Over the years I have hidden certain things from family, friends, and associates. I have been more comfortable standing before others physically naked than I have been baring my soul and exposing my deep thoughts and emotions. I have been afraid for years to be truly seen and heard for who I am beneath the surface, because I feared being judged and wrongly perceived.

I have always been a very anxious person. The anxiety attacks began when I was 10 years old, and I tried very hard to hide them with a strong confident persona. Some days I felt trapped in a body that I did not recognize from head to toe, and I was inside screaming to get out, but no one could hear or understand me. Some days I felt as though I was breaking into a million pieces. I was struggling to hold myself together, but with only two hands I could not fathom how to hold all my fragments together.

Some days I simply did not recognize the face I saw in the mirror, and I would go through those days in a daze, confused and bewildered as to why, when, what, where, which, and how this me came to be me. I struggle with guilt and shame for the decisions I made and the opportunities that I lost. I love people but on tough days I sought seclusion. At times I found it difficult to connect to other people in a loving and acceptable manner as I struggled internally. Because of an inferiority complex, I have so desperately wanted to please others and live up to their standards in life. I felt like a ball in a pinball machine for years trying to please and adhere to the standards of others, and many times it has caused great conflict in relationships. I felt condemned if I did not want to do what they desired. I have dealt with stifled anger, bitterness and unforgiveness due to internal and external conflicts for years.

I have struggled with procrastination and perfectionism, and both have brought great fear and confusion. I had insomnia for years and sometimes drank at night to numb my stressed mind. I have eaten entire cakes and pies in mindless grazing within a day or two. I have been so exhausted that I have sat still for entire days doing nothing and thinking about nothing.

I was afraid to speak about all these buried secrets because I didn't want to be labeled or judged. I was fearful of being criticized and alienated. I have felt lonely while in the presence of others, wanting to connect, but feeling fearful of that connection at the same time. My discernment was lacking at times as I trusted people I should not have trusted perceiving and believing things that were not truthful nor would some things manifest. Secrets are powerful, changing the trajectory of lives as they come to the light as they are spoken and revealed. Buried secrets take root and grow bad fruit as thoughts, ideas, beliefs and personas. Buried secrets also create bitterness and unforgiveness in one's soul, as was my case.

I was angry and beyond PISSED OFF for years, because I did not get what I believed I was entitled to in some areas of life, especially marriage. After my divorce I had to quickly learn how to be the head of my household and handle all the roles that came with that, all while maintaining my role as a woman and mother in my household. I had to figure out how to redefine myself as an individual and professional. I did not have any divorced female friends to lead and guide me through the arduous process of hardships during divorce. I spiraled downward quickly because the foundation of my life was not solid and grounded. I broke down quickly in every area of life; physically, mentally, emotionally, spiritually and financially after my divorce, only discussing it with my counselor and I didn't even have her once my insurance coverage ended.

To top that off, for years my kids and I lived in pre-foreclosure limbo in the house that was awarded to me through my divorce. The mortgage on the house was being sold from mortgage company to mortgage company, which was a blessing and a curse. I endured day after day not knowing our fate with the house because the mortgage was not in my name, so I was not allowed to get any information. I was paying it for a while, trying to figure out how to refinance. After all resources were exhausted, I wondered what would happen to me and my sons from one day to the next day. I tried to have faith that it would work out for our good in spite of how things looked and felt.

I know that depression, mistakes, ignorance, and unconscious living all played a part in my life during this time of being in limbo. I only shared this secret with a few friends in hopes of finding helpful programs to sort out the mortgage mess and in dealing with scam modification programs. I also told some friends to warn or encourage them in their situations and then told a few who I suspected were in the same predicament, but who were keeping it secret too. My hope is that my sharing this will help alert others before they reach crisis mode, and to encourage those who, like me, have been in crisis to persevere through.

I am a part of an epidemic of suburban moms silently struggling to survive and thrive after hardships such as divorce, widowhood, or displacement due to abuse or other reasons. This is a silent epidemic. We are afraid to speak up and admit that we may not fully know how we got into some of the situations in which we find ourselves. We are smart women, but we feel like failures and frauds in so many ways, especially if we have allowed ourselves to be deceived in any way or have settled for less than we deserved in any area of life. When we have lived middle- or upper-income lifestyles, we are so afraid of being judged by our current poverty situations. It is embarrassing, as well as heart wrenching, to explain our predicaments to others who do not understand and cannot empathize. There are sometimes so many variables to our problems that it is difficult to find a workable solution to help us dig out of the very deep pit in which we find ourselves. We feel all alone and without the necessary tools needed to extract ourselves from these situations.

Sudden life changes and quick transitions have side-swiped many suburban moms who are battered and bruised in all areas of life. The problem is that on the surface or from the outside looking in, we appear to be doing fine. Many suburban moms are still living in the lovely or luxury houses they resided in prior-to-divorce, they are still driving decent or luxury cars, but no one sees that the rooms of those houses may be empty. Furniture and jewelry have been sold,_cars are running on fumes, pantries are bare, their wallets are empty, and their bank accounts are in the red.

I was tired of being sick and tired, and I was tired of being alone, afraid to be seen and heard. I am the voice of many suburban moms who sometimes have hungry children and are afraid of becoming homeless, who feel obsolete in the job market after years of being at home raising the kids, and who may have only worked part time for extra or fun money. This is the culmination of my story and the stories of many who crossed my path or the stories they shared with me of their struggling mothers, sisters and girlfriends.

 Now that I have faced my fears and told you my secrets, I want to share my awakening process with you. The purpose of this book is to help women in transition due to illness, divorce, widowhood, displacement, unemployment, under-employment, or self-employment to heal all of their physical, mental, emotional, spiritual and financial hurts. A plan was placed in my heart in 2009 to establish an organization or a ministry to help women like myself and to use this book as a tool to help these women and their children. It is my hope that someday this plan, this vision or blueprint for this ministry, will give financial assistance that serves as a help to keep these previously middle-income women from becoming destitute during their transitional process. My transitional process has taken many years of ups and downs that brought enlightenment and strength to persevere and give birth to this book. Through writing at various times, I was able to look back at my journey as a road map, and I pray you are blessed in some way as you read and contemplate your journey or that of others.

On the eve of my 39th birthday, an awakening in my spirit began my transformation. I read my journal entry that day and remember, feeling sad and questioning my life, looking into the mirror and wondering who this was looking back at me. I was at the worst place in my life, and I began asking various questions of my friends and myself. I wanted to know:

> Is this all my life has to offer?
> What is my passion and purpose?
> Who am I and what do I want from my life?
> Do other women contemplate these same questions?
> Why did I say this or that or do this or that?

I assessed the then-current state of my life. I was lonely, disconnected, depressed, overweight, unhappy, discontent, and I disliked myself most of the time. I had bankrupted my business and I was using my credit cards to pay for my expenses; I was addicted to spending. Alone at night, I drank and ate heavily to comfort myself before going to sleep, praying that tomorrow would be better.

Introduction

Once I started sharing my thoughts and feeling, I realized I was not alone in this awakening_process. Many women embark upon this soul-searching journey around this same age, especially when hardships occur. They are brought to this process as they approach their forties, become discontented with their careers, their significant other, or find they have lost their identity.

In 1994, I had the first of numerous auto accidents. All but 2 of the accidents were rear-end collisions varying from minor to severe, causing the total loss of several cars. I had soft tissue injuries from head to toe over the years. My weight went up and down from medications, inflammation, pregnancies, excess cortisol and chronic dieting. Years later emotional trauma and chronic stress from accidents, divorce, illness, and the downward turn of the real estate market increased the frequency and threshold of my pain. I was broken mentally, physically, emotionally, spiritually, and financially. I had been a real estate broker for years and my business suffered from debilitating stress, depression, mismanagement of finances, plus having to change company names and rebrand after my divorce. As each year passed, my symptoms multiplied, and pain became a daily part of my life. I did not look or feel like me and I felt trapped in my own body. I desperately searched for keys to healing.

I began journaling in 2000 just before the birth of my third son. It was very therapeutic for me to spend a few minutes journaling each day. I later realized it helped me see my own growth and development as well as pitfalls. I found it very helpful to see my life's journey in black and white. My faith was increased by seeing prayers answered in many of my journal entries. My journals were a record of my physical, mental, emotional, spiritual, and financial struggles and triumphs.

During this time, I became very concerned about my health when I was diagnosed with leaky gut syndrome. I had horrible allergy attacks that caused asthma, rashes, hives, and swelling all over. I started noticing how I looked in photos, and as they say, a picture is worth a thousand words. I knew I needed to learn more to heal my body and my life.

Eventually I reached a point where I was in the worst shape of my life as my weight went up and down considerably. I joined a weight loss challenge with a cash prize, which was a great incentive for me. I knew I had to make changes and I thought the monetary prize would help reduce the financial pressure and stress that I was currently enduring. As I began this weight loss challenge, I realized how disconnected I was from my own body. I felt trapped by my physical self. I did not want or know how to connect to this body that I did not recognize emotionally or mentally because I could not understand why I was not getting the results I expected. I had lost about 70 pounds at one point along my journey, but I regained all of it back, and more. This weight loss challenge reconnected me to my body and put me on a path to learning more to heal myself.

My healing journey started with my introduction to essential oils and green products for all areas of my life, including my environment. I sought to learn more about toxins in my home (which was very important since I worked from home). I had noticed that my three sons and I felt ill after cleaning our home. It was not just feeling tired—we would have headaches and feel very fatigued. I was given some green products to try and noticed we no longer had headaches, nor were we fatigued, after cleaning the house. I began researching holistic alternatives to resolve different issues, not just mask symptoms. I was determined to address the root causes of the various symptoms we were experiencing.

My journey to healing and transformation began to get really interesting and exciting. I was desperately seeking knowledge and understanding of my physical, mental, emotional and spiritual connections that I knew were the keys to setting me free from this hurting and sick body that I felt trapped within. Several friends and doctors shared information with me, and I read numerous books as I prayed for the knowledge needed to help my body heal itself as God intended. I spent numerous hours watching, listening, and learning from various sources. I was determined to transform my body, soul, and spirit.

Even though I did not win the weight loss challenge, it proved to be a catalyst that changed my life immensely. I had been writing this book for years, but realized I was stuck in this project because I was stuck and stagnant in my body. As my body started to move and flow, so did my_writing. My spiritual, mental, emotional, and physical transformation became this book you are reading now.

I realized very early in my transformational process that I am not who I was when I started. I wanted to be able to explain to friends and family my transformational process to assist others in healing, too. I need to stress that I had to give myself permission to put my healing as my number one priority in order to achieve my transformation and understand my body, soul, and spirit connections. My new level of awareness ignited a passion and purpose within me to inspire others to be their best, most authentically well, selves.

As I shared my journey, I wanted to enlighten and encourage others to listen to our bodies and our organs, which will be explained in a later chapter. For instance, I was made aware of basic anatomy and scar tissue how our bodies were created to function. My eyes were opened to the connections and the functions of the fascial tissue, which is the cellular matrix, the communicator and translator of the body. This is why it is imperative that we learn the language of our bodies to truly understand the questions we ask ourselves and how we react to experiences in life.

I have been blessed with many experiences in my own chapters and stories, as well as those shared with me by others, which put me on this path of awakening. Over the years, I have expressed a genuine interest in others' lives and issues. Perfect strangers would tell me things that were very personal and secret, which shocked me for a while! I later realized that, over the_years, I also looked to strangers for an unburdening of the weight and pressure of my secrets. In speaking to someone who doesn't know all our past issues, the words spoken are fewer, and seem many times to be less judgmental than if they came from someone we have known and do not want to disappoint.

I am truly amazed by the remarkable women who have crossed my path. Over the years, I have heard many stories of heartbreak, betrayal, violence, abuse, neglect, confusion, depression, overwhelming pressure, as well as triumph of spirit and love. As women, we wear our stories as masks in many layers, allowing only certain people to see under these various layers. Sometimes we break under the weight of all those stories and roles, which become self-imposed prison bars that we peek through and hide behind. We are filled with fear that someone will find out all that we have hidden inside and unjustly judge us. We wear a happy smile and work to stay in character without giving away the truth—that we are lost and dying inside. We come to the realization at some point that we have lost our way, lost our stability, and cannot remember where or when it happened. Counseling was a blessing to me, and my awakening began with learning how to let go and let God. I started writing poetry again after many years, and I learned to use my poetry as therapy to help me let go. My story may be your story, but we really have many stories. When we share our secrets and stories to help others free themselves, we are also freed, layer by layer.

I pray that the culmination of these stories will help others to increase their faith and strengthen their efforts to fulfill their dreams. This book is about the sharing of women's journeys through struggles with abuse, obesity, Attention Deficit Disorder (ADD), Obsessive Compulsive Disorder (OCD), Dissociative Identity Disorder (DID), addictions, depression, fear, finances, careers, relationships, disappointment, displacement, illness, widowhood, and divorce. It is also about triumph, peace, joy, faith, hope and love. Through our journeys we see how our struggles form a pathway of stumbling blocks that become our stepping stones to a prosperous and balanced life. When we honor and are true to our God-given spiritual gifts and talents, we are in harmony and at peace as we were created to be. This is the road map of my journey and the personal struggles and experiences of those who crossed my path, also in search of how to have a spiritually balanced and prosperous life. I have included poems in this book that I wrote during my transitions to help me find my true feelings and gifts, and I pray they help in your journey.

While I have learned many lessons through my awakening years, I found that once my spirit was awakened, I was set free from my secrets and entanglements. I am at peace and filled with immense joy, allowing me to live with passion and purpose. You too can find that peace and feel that immense joy, allowing *you* to live with passion and purpose.

F or as he thinketh in his heart,
so is he.

Proverbs 23:7 (KJV)

Chapter One

~Awakening~

"I believe the brilliance of our sun pales in comparison to the illumination of the collective spirits of women connected on a mission for Jesus Christ."

~Jonquil G.

"I am a true sprouting vine, and the farmer who tends the vine is my Father. He cares for the branches connected to me by lifting and propping up the fruitless branches and pruning every fruitful branch to yield a greater harvest. The words I have spoken over you have already cleansed you. So, you must remain in life-union with me, for I remain in life-union with you. For as a branch severed from the vine will not bear fruit, so your life will be fruitless unless you live your life intimately joined to mine. I am the sprouting vine and you're my branches. As you live in union with me as your source, fruitfulness will stream from within you-but when you live separated from me you are powerless. John 15:1-5 TPT

The missing link in wholeness, healing and transformation is in truly understanding connectivity, wellness, and the link between the two. The Principle of Connectivity is based on the advancement of theories or practices through gradual accumulation of knowledge to assimilate, then solve issues. The Concept of Wellness has for many years been synonymous with health, which loosely implies mental and physical well-being.

Awakening

Wellness is now a buzz word that encompasses more than the traditional ideal of the absence of disease. Today wellness encompasses our minds, bodies, souls, and spirits as well as our environment. Wellness is choosing a positive mindset and a desire to assume responsibility for—or give permission to—yourself to transform and heal as you transition through your life.

Connectivity brings wellness to all our worlds physically, mentally, emotionally, spiritually, and financially. Connectivity brings alignment to our body, soul, and spirit as well as to God as a pathway from earth to heaven. For example, when we accidentally say things that are inappropriate or rude, we cause a disconnection from ourselves, people, places, and things in our lives. It requires connectivity and wellness to create a healthy balance and connection to others and ourselves.

Through experiences, research, and prayer, I developed a deeper understanding of connectivity and wellness. I found so much helpful information while researching, and I gained deeper understanding while praying, which helped me to understand the energy of the body, mental and physical pathways, and the emotional connections linked to each organ. I was introduced to numerous people or teachers over the years who were very instrumental in my healing and transformational journey. I learned how to interpret the language and signals my body was sending me and I began to understand the importance of listening to my body. I also learned to listen to the language and signals from the bodies of others to assist them in finding well-being.

I realized that I developed a better understanding of some things after hearing or reading other works, such as *Switch on Your Brain* by Dr. Caroline Leaf. I have read countless articles and books on wellness and healing modalities. Over the years, I found that seeds were planted in my mind and then watered and fertilized by prayer and additional information that was introduced to me. Then many times I would read or listen to the information again and again to gain depth of knowledge. I also found confirmation of insight gained while doing experiments or exercises I came across or were divinely gained. I see energy and connections to people, places, and things like a matrix of spider webs. These intrinsically designed pathways and points of connection, create structure as God's master plan for each of our lives. This matrix of spider webs is woven with points of connection bringing form and clear vision as we go through life expressing our free will to lead or be lead. It is amazing that I saw the same correlating patterns within the human body when looking at the fascia and connective tissue structure and its connections to different parts of the body.

The physical world of the body is connected through the fascia or fascial tissue, which is the thin, white flexible connective tissue that encompasses collagen and forms a sheath over everything within the body from head to toe. This fascial tissue and structural matrix of the body translates and communicates its electro-chemical language like a subway system, carrying packages of information or instructions to and from various locations throughout our bodies. The cells are seeds, building blocks of energy, which grow into thoughts. Those thoughts then grow into things both positive and negative, depending on your mindset and the nature of the packages of information or instructions transitioning through the body from minute to minute and day to day.

The matrix of the fascia or connective tissue of the body forms the pathways for connectivity and healing from top to bottom and inside-out. God intended the body to heal itself, and this matrix is used for that purpose. It is fascinating that the womb, the center of creation, has been referred to biblically as the matrix of the womb. Everything in the body from nerves, joints, bones, and organs are covered in and connected to fascia.

The frame of the body has either a loose or tight fascial structure that forms the framework for posture and positioning of internal organs and tissues. The fascial tissue has a role in metabolism, waste removal, and fighting infections. Scar tissue and fascial adhesions are the result of our bodies' natural healing process, and it occurs both internally and externally. The process of wound repair causes scarring to different degrees, replacing the normal skin or other tissue, leaving it less functional as it was originally before the injury, trauma, car accident, or abuse. A scar from childhood can spread in different directions and restrict proper movement and body function.

When injuries happen to the body, the fascia tissue is very sensitive to the pain, and a vicious cycle begins. This brutal cycle of illness can begin with chronic pain and allergies, causing an imbalance of good bacteria, yeast, and parasite over-growth, which progresses to leaky gut and increased sensitivity to food. This in turn can lead to a weakened immune system depleted of vitamins, minerals, and key nutrients, resulting in scarring within the digestive system. If the connective tissue becomes scar tissue (which can form on the inside of the body in and on the joints or organs, as well as on the skin) a lifetime of complications and pain may persist. Scar tissue is formed at or near the site of injuries, surgeries, or disease to indicate damaged tissue; it is like a cast that the body creates to protect itself. Scarring is created during the healing process, but its fibrous nature interferes with balance and limits blood supply to, and functions of, the involved tissues, nerves, joints, and organs. Even though connective tissue once damaged becomes scar tissue, it miraculously serves us well as it helps knit us together again in order to mend and heal. Over-production of scar tissue during the healing process can not only restrict_movement, but also the flow of energy through the body, contributing to additional pain. It is important to know that scarring is good for healing but special care and techniques are needed to make sure full movement and energy flow is restored to renew the body for optimal well-being.

All parts and systems in the body are interconnected, and if dysfunction exists in an area—ranging from temporary pain to long-term damage--other areas can be negatively impacted. If you close a tunnel or pathway and the subway train cannot go to that area, then alternate routes are needed, which is what happens within the body when pathways are blocked by scar tissue. Learning to be in tune with and understanding the connections and communication systems of the body empowers us to take responsibility for our healing and inspire others to do the same.

The God-given gift of connectivity is the interconnected systems of people, places, things, and our bodies (body, soul and spirit). It is being in the right place, at the right time, to serve the right people or to be served. It is based on a supportive system of like energies being drawn together to manifest dreams, desires, plans, purposes, missions, and movements. Supporting and connecting structures form matrixes, which are the points of connectivity for our worlds in every aspect of life—physically, mentally, emotionally, spiritually, and financially. When we are well, we are able to show up, serve, and connect for an intentional purpose. Within this connectivity, our ability to be seen for who we are in a particular season of life affects the size and balance of our world.

It takes great courage to be truly transparent in the physical world. You feel stripped bare and in the spotlight for all the world to see. In the physical world, that which is on the surface is seen by the public, and at different times we will and are able to display different talents and parts of ourselves. It is ironic that we can be confident in certain places with certain people and things, but feel totally inadequate, incompetent and lack confidence in some places with some people due to past triggers or old wounds and scars, especially when pain remains attached to some memories.

The mental world has its own nuances revealed through connectivity in our various networks. As we spend time with others, there are some things about us which become apparent. Some things remain a mystery to us until we are ready and willing to accept feedback. At, times we run on automatic and are not aware of our reactions, movements, words and behaviors. There are also times when we seem to be outside ourselves, listening and watching as though someone else spoke the words or performed the actions we just witnessed. We find that we are puzzled as to what caused us to behave that way. It requires self-exploration, and assistance may be needed to help us get to the root cause of the behavior. As we begin to connect the points, we connect our worlds for balance and wellness. In doing so, we create an outline of our new story and our new self which moves, speaks, and behaves differently than our old self.

The brain cells store and send information. It's like secrets being quietly passed through our mental world to the cells stored in our organs, and these cells are connected to specific emotions, energies, hormones, and frequencies. These pathways of flowing secrets help formulate the words, thoughts, and intentions of our characters or roles played in our daily lives from season to season, line by line, chapter by chapter. The secrets are played out by each character within us from day to day as we show up in masks and costumes and help us write or live out the story of our lives.

The connections made in each world physically, mentally, emotionally, and spiritually formulate the reactions, tolerances, and nuances of each character role or personality trait. Our heart-mind-brain connection bridges or connects our worlds as the heart, brain and gut connect with one another. If the thoughts, intentions, and motives of the heart are negative, the gut is affected. Then the brain causes the release of hormones or brain chemicals that seek to restore balance or harmony to the body, soul, and spirit. All your thoughts and characteristics, balanced or unbalanced, are a reflection of and a part of you, making you unique and different through all the seasons of your life. Your expressed uniqueness blesses the universe with your special talents and gifts.

The emotional world is where we are truly seen and heard by those who share that season with us. When we lose control of our emotions, we may shock ourselves and others with our reactions towards people or circumstances. We need help with our emotional world because these are our blind spots, and these blind spots or errors of the tongue are sometimes referred to as Freudian slips. We rarely explore the root cause of these errors and their interconnectedness to emotional issues, or masks worn in our lives, without being asked to by someone assisting us in healing. If we are willing to be courageous and spend time exploring who we are emotionally, we will become our best and most authentic selves. Those slips of the tongue are guideposts. But many times, we cannot see what's there without it being pointed out by others. Those incidents can be compared to accumulated onion layers that stick together. Peeling those layers requires hard work to dig in and excavate. Finally arriving at the root cause is where we find our wellness. Dealing with the root causes of weaknesses, brokenness and Freudian slips exposes things that must be addressed for peace of mind and heart. Once the root causes are exposed, we can see and hear who we really are at our core as we change and evolve, maturing emotionally, mentally becoming more enlightened, and prayerfully more accepting of ourselves.

In the spiritual world, we find unknown things to explore, and intuition springs from this world. In this world we tap into the unknown and make discoveries about ourselves, others, and the outside worlds, visible and invisible. Connectivity from the spiritual world gives new meaning to life and many times turns your worlds topsy-turvy. Once the onset of enlightenment begins, your physical, mental, and emotional worlds are never the same. The matrix becomes visible; a grand design for your life, with points of connection from you to yourself, to the people, places, and things you desire in the past, present, and future. We are awakened and, if we rely on and trust our intuition, we flow with ease from world to world, point to point, and line to line, connecting and reconnecting, becoming well and aware.

It is imperative we understand the God-given gift of connectivity to help empower others and ourselves to heal. Learning to be more in tune to the body and its communication system puts us in a position to receive guidance from the Creator of our world, as He utilizes the huge percentage of our minds not normally accessed in daily life. Wellness and connectivity require bravery to find our healthy, authentic selves. We must give ourselves permission to simply BE!

The heart plays a big part in our physical and spiritual lives and is the source of those slips of the tongue. Everything affects the balance of the heart, our center for love and joy. When we are under a lot of stress, an imbalance or disconnection occurs between the mind and body. We speak from that state of being. In holding grudges and being offended by others, we are unknowingly holding them captive in our joyless hearts, which adds to the imbalance and disconnection.

The financial world affects all the other worlds. In turn, our finances can be affected negatively by imbalances of the physical, mental, emotional, and spiritual worlds. When we are physically ill or unable to work for various reasons, our financial budget may be thrown off balance. When we have negative thoughts, use negative words, have emotional outbursts, irrational behavior, and carry unforgiveness, our finances are just as affected as other aspects of our lives. We become stuck in old roles, positions or levels, which cause our financial world to also suffer. In addition, lack of faith and limiting beliefs, as well as spiritual attacks, can also work against us. Understanding where we are and the level of authenticity in all our worlds determines where we are in all areas of life, including our finances.

Some people have to reinvent, transform, regenerate, and develop new roles or characteristics as well as new ideas, endeavors, and businesses as they write new chapters for the stories of their lives. As we seek to clear our hearts and minds of negativity, old fragmented character roles, thoughts, and intentions, we stop sleepwalking and functioning on autopilot. In the process of awakening, we develop a new mindset and speech; we start asking different questions, creating strategies of positive change and growth in all areas of life. This will bring balance to the interconnected worlds of our bodies, souls, and spirits.

Chapter Two

~What's In A Question?~

"There are years that ask questions and years that answer..."

~Zora Neale Hurston

Then the Lord spoke to Job out of the storm. He said: "Who is this that obscures my plans with words without knowledge? Brace yourself like a man; I will question you, and you shall answer me." Job 38:1-3 TPT

A question is an inquiry, something that can provide the catalyst for answers to our issues and problems, and in turn, help us determine our choices and be an avenue to insight. Questions have existed since the beginning of everything. Religions and philosophies come and go, but questions will continue. They are needed for awakening, growth, development, transformation, and transition. The soul is both intrigued and overwhelmed by questions that arise. The more disconnected and confused we feel, the more overwhelmed we become with each unanswered question. Disappointing and unsatisfactory answers can affect the way we see ourselves in a particular season of life. Why, what, when, where, who, and how will awaken your soul as you begin with asking and seeking questions about yourself, such as: what is the meaning of my name and how does it encompass the essence of myself?

I believe that from birth to our thirties are the years of asking questions, and the forties onward are the years that we answer them. It is by no means easy to get to those answers; we become engaged in a physical and spiritual battle when we seek them. During the years of answers, we awaken and come into a knowing of who we are when alone. Once we learn to be still and listen to the answers within, we are able to uncover our authentic selves. This knowing of things becomes instinctive in matters that previously eluded us. The elements of our stories that cause us the most discomfort help to fashion our character. During those early years we become filled with questions about why life felt difficult and when our expectations went unmet. As we became overwhelmed with questions, we felt more alone and confused.

Questions help us to be vulnerable and naked, to expose our true self, to uncover strengths and be free from negative entanglements, and to embrace positive entanglements or connections. Our experiences add to who we become, thereby increasing our knowledge and wisdom. The sum total of our experiences makes us more empathetic. We also develop perseverance during difficult circumstances. The transparency we display during difficult circumstances is a signpost confirming the strength gained and willingness to show our authenticity in that season.

The ability to ask the right questions has been the key to the success of interviewers, like Barbara Walters, as well as great counselors. There is an art to asking the right questions of ourselves and others. As we master this art with ourselves, we are then equipped to master it with others. As we ask questions, we move forward on our journey, seeking and finding information that helps us make decisions and choices that are in alignment with our true nature and character. These questions and answers bring about transparency and comfort with our identity, moving us forward physically, mentally, emotionally, spiritually, and financially. These answers help with decisions to move us forward or backward, as well as helping us to take a stand on who we are at that point in our journey.

Beliefs regarding failures determine our questions and decisions. For instance, if we see ourselves as failures, we start to see ourselves as obsolete and lacking in skills needed to transition in all areas of our life. Myths and negative beliefs can keep us in a state of constant questioning and confusion. We may feel inadequate, think we lack the ability to make good decisions, feel unsuccessful, and think negatively when circumstances are difficult. But those are false beliefs. Failures are, in essence, a feedback system that we can use to change our decisions, direction and associations, putting us on new paths to new beginnings even changing our thoughts from negative to positive.

It is difficult to find our joy and peace until we realize that it is found in the answers that we seek from ourselves, others and God. These answers help us redefine ourselves as we use our gifts and talents. Our joy and peace show up when we trust ourselves and God. Our passion and purposes are also revealed in the found answers. It is so important that we find the answers, the guideposts to our passion and purpose, in order to live in alignment with our destiny, to find satisfaction with our lives, and bring to the world our gifts and talents to bless others. We become dissatisfied with life and question what our life has to offer when we are out of alignment with the plan God has for us. When we choose to live a life based on the goals, desires, choices, decisions, and beliefs of others we war within ourselves due to misalignment. Connections to people with negative thoughts and beliefs can cloud our judgement and hinder our progress in different seasons of life. We start to feel like captives in prisons without bars, as we allow the words, thoughts, and stories of others to become our narrative. They dictate our goals, desires, choices, decisions and their beliefs are accepted, to keep peace in relationships. Some relationships will have to be renegotiated and re-evaluated to live according to the plans and purposes that God has for us.

If you keep a list of goals, it is very encouraging when you achieve those goals. In seeking to live a life of my desire, I found over the years that successful people create their success by doing various things. Many stated that positive thinking was of the utmost importance, and it has been proven by doctors and scientists alike. For example, Dr. Caroline Leaf spoke of positive thinking in her book *Switch on Your Brain.* It is amazing how science is catching up to what is written in the Bible, such as this amazing verse below which comes from the book of Habakkuk. And then GOD answered: "Write this. Write what you see. Write it out in big block letters so that it can be read on the run. This vision-message is a witness pointing to what's coming. It aches for the coming—it can hardly wait! And it doesn't lie. If it seems slow in coming, wait. It's on its way. It will come right on time. Habakkuk 2:2-3 (MSG)

The imagination is also very important in visualizing the desires of our heart and then seeing them actually manifest. We must then know that we have the courage to act and achieve those goals by using our talents. It takes twenty-one days to create a habit and working to achieve our goals requires that we create habits that will help us accomplish and sustain those goals. It is imperative that we keep these wise sages close to our hearts to find signposts with why, what, when, where, who, and how. These will guide us on our journey to our destiny.

During times of goal setting, we need to think of the questions and the answers, especially why. Then visualize connections and possible pathways to achieve those goals. Next, visualize how things will look and feel for ourselves and our loved ones when we achieve our goals. Visualization is so powerful! It is seeing what we have written down when goal setting. As we visualize with a joyful heart there is the connecting of energy to the people, places, and things needed to accomplish the plan and purpose for our life.

It is also imperative that we have a thankful and cheerful heart filled with gratitude for the blessings we have had, the ones we have now, and those on the way. Gratitude increases our joy and faith and helps to improve physical attributes and our health, with improved cellular function and better sleep as benefits. Visualization and the use of our imagination to form pathways is one of the most powerful gifts that we have been given. The more we train it, the more amazing and aware we become in all of our worlds or areas of life.

 Along with visualization, forgiveness is essential to being a blessing to ourself and others. There are times when we need to visualize forgiving someone, either because they are deceased, cannot be found, or simply because it is better for us to forgive them privately to keep from causing more issues for ourself or for them. Our spirit knows what is best when it comes to forgiveness (which is for you), and decides we are ready to forgive and let go. As mentioned previously, it is not good to hold a grudge or unforgiveness in our heart because we are holding people captive. How many people are held captive within you?

Our list of goals serves as a checklist of achievements and gives us objectives that redirect us when we get off track and lose our direction. By keeping lists and checking off those goals, we see our progress and answered prayers in black and white. Perseverance is continuously taking the action needed to achieve one's goals no matter what happens, an attribute which builds character, and that character builds hope for an amazing future for ourselves and others. We will find that development and growth occur when answers are found. It is this checklist of achievements that keeps us moving forward and connected, becoming more awakened with each transition and transformation.

In the process of gaining answers from God, we go through several stages of growth, as well as encountering and experiencing more of God. The answers we gain form the roadmap of where we have been in life and with God. In receiving answers on our journey, we are guided down the path by the direction we take or should take as revealed to us as we pray and travel through life. The knowledge gained helps us grow and continue to transition.

This newfound knowledge helps us to help others grow and develop, as well. Together, we and our partners in transition will progress more quickly because we guide and encourage one another along our journeys. We are also able to hear the voices of our partners, teachers, tutors, and mentors in our head as we progress, giving us positive feedback to help us develop during difficult times. Community with like-minded people is so important to help us transition and transform more easily and to keep us in our lane or on the right course.

We are sometimes our own worst enemy when it comes to our health, growth, and development. We get stuck in our bodies and souls, slowing our progress and, in many cases, becoming ill, confused, and incapable of making good decisions due to low self-esteem and other issues, such as our own negative self-talk. We sometimes misinterpret the intentions of others when our souls are confused, and we become stuck instead of growing in many areas of life. It is easy to make assumptions about others when we have been spoken to in a negative manner, either by others or ourselves. We unconsciously mirror behavior that we have seen and heard in the past, then reflect onto others what we have erroneously chosen to believe about ourselves and about them. We separate ourselves from others when we have convinced ourselves we are unworthy to be in the presence of certain people, especially positive successful people. In separating from them, our negative self-talk increases, in many cases due to a lack of connection with these same people. It is easier to learn and implement new behaviors when surrounded by positive people, affirming us as we fellowship. Affirmations help to change our energy and essence. They also help to change our speech and our emotions, enabling the implementation of new habits and behaviors.

Answers direct you to your next steps, but without the right questions, the answers cannot be found. Those answers also connect us to others, show us what we need, and open our mind and heart to all the possibilities and blessings around us. But we have to ask the right questions to get to the right answers. In getting the right answers, we are placed on the right path, in the right place, with the right people, at the right time. Answers reveal we are all on a journey together, connecting us at various intersections.

By asking and seeking knowledge over the years, I have written this book and one of poetry. My energy aligned with that of like-minded others on the same journey of writing books. I was also intrigued as I connected to others on exploration through the physical, mental, emotional, spiritual, and financial worlds, as we sought to understand the matrix and connections that go through all these worlds. It was a blessing to come alongside like-minded others on a quest, asking each other questions to gain more clarity and solutions to whatever ails us. There is a spiritual solution to every problem, and it points us towards God, our source. As we ask questions, we bring forth answers to problems, and we transition from awakening to awareness. Becoming aware reveals chains and masks that hold us captive and we are greatly blessed as like-minded divine connections help us gain freedom.

Chapter Three

~Removing The Masks~

"There is no agony like bearing an untold story inside of you."

~Maya Angelou

Are you weary, carrying a heavy burden? Come to me. I will refresh your life, for I am your oasis. Simply join your life with mine. Learn my ways and you'll discover that I'm gentle, humble, easy to please. You will find refreshment and rest in me. For all that I require of you will be pleasant and easy to bear. Matthew 11:28-30 TPT

Why do we wear masks? Masks are used to cover, conceal, protect, restrain, and disguise. Masks come in different sizes, shapes, and forms. Many questions and answers are hidden behind and centered on our various masks. A mask is used to block the view of something, keep a secret, or conceal one's real identity, personality, character traits, or intentions. Accompanying some masks are chains and baggage that hinder growth, development, and the ability to get to root causes of pain, trauma, hindrance, and confusion in various areas of life. Emotions are also hidden behind masks and keep us connected to people, places, and things from which we may need to disconnect. Senses are blurred by masks, and they conceal things physically, mentally, emotionally, spiritually, and financially, such as when we are smiling but are secretly miserable inside.

Some examples of masks are makeup to hide bruises inflicted by an abuser. Some masks are pretending to be happy to pacify a narcissist, especially in public. Masks are used both to deceive and to protect for preservation. Masks prevent true growth and personal development as well as professional development. Masks get in the way of transparency and authenticity. Many try to fake it until they make it but that certainly does not work long term in a marriage, because after a while the weight of the façade of the many masks will fall down for all to see the smokescreen hiding a bad marriage.

We are responsible for the masks we put on that were given to us by others when we accept their opinions or beliefs as our truth. Masks diminish our passion and distract us from our God-given purposes, missions, and talents. We sometimes take on certain characters or roles in our efforts at trying to please others. We also take on roles when we believe those roles or characters are ideally who we should be in certain seasons.

Sometimes our true personality or nature conflicts with the character that we've chosen to play. These roles that we play are like the masks or costumes that we wear, just like the costumes worn by children playing make-believe. Some of the personalities that we play are chosen by us, some are given to us, and some are forced upon us. We learn different things from the different roles that we play or masks that we wear. Sometimes those lessons come easy and feel natural, but sometimes they come very hard and costly.

Many lessons, easy or hard, are unfortunately learned in hindsight after playing different roles, wearing some masks, or personifying certain names. If we truly understood the names that were given to us at birth (or even those names that God later chose for us as we were renamed), we would know the meanings of our names, directing us to who we are supposed to be. Our character and personality lie within our name; our name encompasses our identity, character, and essence.

The roles, masks, and chains that we end up wearing change so many areas of life, including our beliefs and belief systems. Those belief systems are given to us from our parents, peers, business partners, and husbands. Sometimes we forget that we have a choice in what we believe; many times, those beliefs dictate the roles that we will play in different seasons of our lives. As we become more enlightened, we update our belief systems to be more in alignment with the roles or masks that we've chosen to wear in these various seasons. In looking at our beliefs, we find the connections and root causes of negative thinking and failures we've gone through, as well as triumphs and successes. Our beliefs sometimes trap us, and we begin a long chain of secrets, lies, and addictions if we play out certain roles while feeling guilty and ashamed. These disguises hide our souls, and we need to remove them to regain our integrity, to find our authenticity and real beauty.

I found that the key to finding me came in the form of writing in my journal and writing poetry. My writing saved me in more ways than I can imagine; it was a cleansing of my soul each time I put pen to paper. I believe that that after I started my first journal, I could see in black and white the characters and different personalities that I played in various seasons. During the process of awakening and cleansing my soul, I saw patterns in my behavior and vices that I picked up along the way. When we eliminate a character or vice from our lives, our minds and hearts, we mourn for that loss as one would mourn a lost lover. It is imperative that we replace the eliminated vices with healthy, positive habits in order to prevent the negative things and any new "foes" from reinvading our hearts and minds. These foes, cohorts and legions of depression, addiction, pain and hopelessness many times come back into one's cleansed soul to reoccupy space like someone moving in and out of a summer residence season after season.

We take on different learned behaviors or habits when we play certain characters for long periods of time. Some of those characteristics are those which others expect of us, which are sometimes out of alignment with who we are at our core. Some of these behaviors are learned, based on codependency with other characters in our lives from childhood. We learn how to play various character roles from those of influence that were constantly around us. The cause and effect of some of those learned behaviors are carried with us for many years. These destructive behaviors, which come from control and manipulation, learned at an early age, teach us what defines power and strength according to our influencers. These lessons regarding power and strength dictate who we become and how we use control. Those of us who have not learned any other way to accomplish certain goals will become frustrated. That frustration turns us to what we learned in childhood and how to use control and manipulation to help us rise to the top.

Some reciprocal relationships trap us into wearing masks to create connections and balance in relationships. We sometimes take on characters that bring balance to the other person and find codependency in those roles. It is great when a positive, synergistic relationship exists. Then both people are respected and admired for their true essences.

On the other hand, we can wind up putting on masks that are out of alignment with who we are when we have negative, codependent relationships. Those who develop a need to please are always concerned with the opinions that others have of them. In order to have reciprocal relationships, some will continue to give and give until nothing is left, believing lies and pretending all is well. But they cannot see the very essence of who they really are, especially if there were many controlling relationships filled with criticism in their past. We put on masks, we carry baggage, and we remain in chains to satisfy the expectations of others. Even as children we learned to put on masks and take on roles to either protect someone else or in hopes of protecting ourselves. For example, some kids learn to remain quiet and seek to be invisible to keep from drawing the attention of the abuser in their home. They learn and embody certain characteristics just to survive and many continue playing these characters throughout their lives for survival. Some develop a nak for duplicitous characteristics behaving totally opposite from one environment to another like an on stage and back stage persona.

Many times, fear is the root cause of why we play certain roles. We are sometimes fearful of being exposed for who we really are at our core. If we have low self-esteem, the fear of being wrongly judged for who we are at our very core is more than we feel we can handle. So much time and energy are used concealing our identities from others in some way, due to the fear of who we were in the past or may become in the future. Many of us remain in hiding, living as chameleons, afraid of our own nature and nakedness, afraid to show others any part of ourselves that is unique and different. We are so afraid to expose our sometimes-crazy thoughts, beliefs, and behaviors and to be judged and rejected. The thought of being rejected by someone (especially if we already see ourselves as different and are desperate to fit in), causes us to gladly play whatever role is expected of us to feel accepted. It is sad that those of us who struggle most with judgment and rejection find ourselves inflicting judgment and rejection upon others. We are afraid to embrace the magnitude of our true power and influence that can occur when we let our lights shine to be truly seen by others.

We sometimes allow the magnitude of issues placed upon our shoulders to overshadow our true power. We find ourselves buckling at the knees and worrying about everything. In some roles we are given the responsibility of repairing or fixing issues for others and neglect our personal responsibility to ourselves. When we do not set boundaries, and worse, do not clearly state those boundaries to others, we take on more responsibility, shame, blame, and guilt than is rightfully ours.

Broken people do not take responsibility for their part in their being broken adults, nor do they eagerly seek to mend and repair from childhood. Many broken people will not openly admit to being broken, and will wear masks to hide their cracks, gaping holes, and chasms. We cannot change the broken and dysfunctional childhoods and pasts, but we are each responsible for choosing wellness and becoming whole adults. Denial, guilt, and shame traps us into remaining in character and on stage with our masks, and if we have walked in a role for a long time, we may have forgotten who we really are or who we should be at certain times in life. Good or bad, we play roles to serve a purpose either for ourselves or for others. We also play roles to gain acceptance or praise. As I stated earlier, some roles are given to us and we freely choose to take them on, and some are forced upon us based on our need to meet the expectations of these people or the need of an individual or group whom we desire to be connected to.

Sometimes in life, things do not go as we expect them to, and we have to accept things as they are so that transformation and growth can happen. We must hear our voice in our heads above all others and combine it with faith. We look to the future, especially when the events of life have been unpleasant. We sometimes find ourselves in cycles of reliving the same or similar unpleasant events over and over again. We must ask ourselves: what must we learn in these unpleasant present moments of life? We many times fail to grasp the epiphany that how we deal with the present moment affects the future. If we seek to find the meaning or lesson in the discomfort of the past, present or future, we will develop the understanding that it all connects seamlessly. Divine moments occur when the future is now, and we experience and embrace everything that life has to teach us. These moments define us and grow us in all areas of life, in all roles or characters. Those masks are then used to serve a higher purpose (when we understand the power of our influence) by sharing our lessons learned.

We learn very valuable lessons that serve a higher purpose when it is our intention to use everything to grow and develop and assist others in their growth process. It is so very important that we understand that we are entitled to our feelings, whether they be happy, sad, or angry. It is imperative that we are mindful of our actions as well as the reactions to our feelings and their effects on our worlds.

For example, we don't realize how unhappy we are when we are carrying around excess weight as a disguise. When we shed weight, we remove the excess mass, which is our costume on the outside. Many times, it takes longer to shed the effects of the weight on the inside, unless it is dealt with spiritually. Many times, it takes longer for the emotions to come into alignment, especially if we have not made the connection or found the root cause for the excess mass. Some people get drawn back in and regain the weight, trying to please others, because once they have removed that costume of weight, they are no longer in alignment with their friends or family. Some roles, as I said earlier, were given to us, and if we are the fat person in the group, then when we have a new look and new attitude, we also take on a new role. Our friends may not know how to deal with the new person we have become.

We all have roles that we take on or that were given to us within the circles that we connect to, but we have free will to choose to accept or deny those roles. Just because we may have chosen to accept a role in the past does not mean we must continue in that role in the present. Role playing brings about growth and development. Practice helps us better play the characters that we have chosen to portray in different seasons of life. We must work at being good in the roles that we choose to play. It is so important that we remain mindful of removing masks or costumes that no longer serve us well in new seasons. Creating newness in any area of life requires us to take inventory of each area, then make changes which embrace the new, as well as bring balance to our worlds. It takes great soul searching and digging beneath the many layers of masks under which we find buried our true identity; which is our treasure. As we take responsibility for the choices we made or allowed to be made for us, we learn from them. As we seek to learn we can change our lives and find balance as well as peace in the freedom of our personal free will and choices.

We need to understand that success and identity are not numbers on a scale. Success and identity are also not a credit score or the number of dollars that we have in the bank. It is not about the overwhelming expectations to be daughters, sisters, mothers, wives, or businesswomen, we may experience at times nor should our success in these roles dictate our true identity as children of God. The roles, characters, or masks we wear become heavy burdens when we do not know how to strip down to our essence and be seen, clearly exposed and uncovered by ourselves and others.

We all desire to be truly seen and accepted by others the way that God sees us, and ultimately, to be truly loved by others the way that God loves us. Removing the masks is very difficult; it requires rebuilding relationships and searching for our buried treasure. The thought of possibly sacrificing relationships if we refuse to continue playing certain roles expected of us, especially in relationships that we have had for many years, fills us with fear. We become weary from the weight of all of our baggage, chains, and masks. Our soul desires to be set free, unbridled, and joyfully exposed. Once our soul has awakened, we stop sleepwalking and become aware, exposing our connections to God and our worlds physically, mentally, emotionally, spiritually, and financially, ushering in more love, joy, peace, and triumphs than we ever imagined were possible.

~You Don't Know The Cost Of Her Smile!~

Can you see that my smile says the joy of the Lord is my strength?

Can you see that my eyes say I know the plans He has for me, plans to prosper me and not to harm me?

I smile because I am happy, I smile because I am free, I smile because He broke chains off me.

There is buried treasure in earthen vessels; listen closely as I pour out mine without measure.

There is buried treasure in earthen vessels hidden behind victorious smiles and tear-filled eyes.

I cry out in joy, I cry out in glee, I cry out because He poured out His mercy and grace upon me.

Do you know when you are looking at a woman of worship, courage, and faith?

Do you know the cost of my smile or her smile or her smile?

What is the cost of Mary's smile as she worships at the feet of Jesus and pours out her tears and the oil from her prized alabaster box?

Can you tell me the cost of broken bones sustained from the one who was supposed to protect and love you?

Can you tell me the cost of desire that's been lost in a marital bed that felt dead, which now holds one instead of two?

Can you tell me the cost when hopes been lost in daily misuse and abuse?

I smile because I am happy, I smile because I am free, I smile because He broke chains off me.

There is buried treasure in earthen vessels; listen closely as I pour out mine without measure.

There is buried treasure in earthen vessels hidden behind victorious smiles and tear-filled eyes.

I cry out in joy, I cry out in glee, I cry out because He poured out His mercy and grace upon me.

What is the cost of Deborah's smile as she courageously leads men into battle?

Can you tell me the cost when you know that who you were has been lost?

Can you tell me the cost of homes and financial resources that have been lost?

Can you tell me the cost when good health has been lost?

I smile because I am happy, I smile because I am free, I smile because He broke chains off me.

There is buried treasure in earthen vessels listen closely as I pour out mine without measure.

There is buried treasure in earthen vessels hidden behind victorious smiles and tear-filled eyes.

I cry out in joy, I cry out in glee, I cry out because He poured out His mercy and grace upon me.

Do you know when you are looking at a woman of worship, courage, and faith?

Do you know the cost of my smile or her smile or her smile?

What is the cost of Esther's smile as she stepped out in faith to save her people?

Can you see that my smile says I know Jehovah-Jireh, the Lord my provider?

Can you see that my eyes say I know Jehovah-Rapha, the Lord my healer?

I smile because I am happy, I smile because I am free, I smile because He broke chains off me.

There is buried treasure in earthen vessels; listen closely as I pour out mine without measure.

There is buried treasure in earthen vessels hidden behind victorious smiles and tear-filled eyes.

I cry out in joy, I cry out in glee, I cry out because He poured out His mercy and grace upon me.

Before you sneer and criticize, cheer and recognize a woman of worship, courage and faith; pays a cost to smile victoriously with tear-filled eyes and hope upon her face as she seeks His grace.

You don't know the weight of my cross or the number of burdens that I carried, because I was unequally yoked to the one, I chose and married.

You don't know the cost of her worship, courage, and faith and the value of the treasure if left buried behind the tear-stained but smiling face.

You don't know the cost of her smile, but He does as He pours out his infinite mercy and grace!

by Jonquil G

Chapter Four

~When Enough is Enough~

"When you understand the power, you possess by declaring it daily, little by little, you will begin to create a life of power."

~Cindy Trimm

Don't continue to team up with unbelievers in mismatched alliances, for what partnership is there between righteousness and rebellion? Who could mingle light with darkness? 2 Corinthians 6:14 TPT

In the process of removing masks layer by layer, we awaken to the depths of the matrix of connections to the people, places, and things in our lives. We get new and different questions and answers with each stage of growth and layer of removal. We become disappointed during our development and the development of others when relationships do not improve, grow, and change as we had hoped. We disconnect and reconnect to certain people, checking to see if we are now equally yoked or in alignment.

Disappointment affects us physically, mentally, emotionally, spiritually, and financially. Stress and disappointment are the root causes of dis-ease in the mind, body, and soul, as well as the precursor to chronic issues, disease, and dysfunctional relationships. The emotional and mental concerns caused by disappointment and stress are various degrees of anger, fear, depression, brain fog, insomnia, mood swings, and anxiety, just to name a few. Physical issues arise with digestion, fatigue, blood pressure, heart palpitations, as well as autoimmune conditions and chronic pain. These issues all go hand in hand with stress and disappointment with various connections that affect all areas of our lives. We will discuss more of the effects of stress and healing in a later chapter.

Deep seated fear sets in with stress and disappointment, affecting us spiritually and financially too. We become fearful when we are not able to trust God, others, or ourselves, and we become disappointed in the circumstances of life. When fear becomes a part of our mindset, it encroaches on every area of life and distorts our thinking, forming a web of lies that becomes our on and off-stage presence of the many characters within us. This web of lies dictates our struggles with weight, illness, abuse, work, and all relationships. The realization that we are not in alignment with what we are telling ourselves and others means we are ready to really see who we have become and to see the destruction we have caused and/or allowed over time. When we become sick and tired of being in pain in our minds, bodies, and souls, we become driven to find solutions to whatever ails us. In the book *The Lies We Believe* by Dr. Chris Thurman you'll find great suggestions for finding your truth in various circumstances, allowing you to heal your wounds and become whole.

I believe my mindset held me captive in many ways. Along my journey I have met many other captives over the years. My search for healing and freedom has been a blessing, allowing me to connect to some amazing people to learn valuable life lessons and gather information that would help me and others. We have so many different struggles in our human existence, and we need help finding our way to healing all areas of our lives. When we lose our way in the battlefields of life and find ourselves stuck in a trench, we must give ourselves permission to ask for, and then continue to seek, the kind of help that we need. Many times, only those who have been set free are able to recognize those who are stuck and those still oblivious to their trenches or chains.

Sometimes when we get in a trench for protection and we stay there to long because of fear, we forget there is a big, wonderful world out there that offers better or more comfortable ways to live. There are some lessons that we are destined to experience, and our testimonies are then used to help others learn and grow. When we are in transition due to divorce, widowhood, job loss, illness, or decreased income, it is wonderful to find assistance that does not make us feel more broken and worthless after asking for help. It is a blessing to get assistance from people who empower when helping during transitions to make it smoother. It is amazing the difference a year makes when we are in transition, when we can look back at our journey and see all that we have made it through with the kindness of others. That insight then helps us become decisive, stronger, wiser, and more resilient.

After opening our eyes and seeking answers, the process of removing masks is truly about making decisions and prioritizing our lives. At the point when we decide we are done being sick and tired of being sick and tired, angry, battered, and bewildered, we figure out our priorities and start aligning our minds and hearts. In speaking to many women of different ages before, during, and after transitions, I observed that in the moment their hearts and minds align, they found the strength to move forward with conviction in their decisions, priorities, and missions. For some of us it takes a lot of back and forth, a lot of mental and emotional gymnastics, especially when we are trying to please others or are afraid of being judged for our decisions, priorities, and missions.

As I stated previously, some of us are responsible for putting on masks that were given to us when we accept the opinions or beliefs of well-meaning people in our lives as our truth. We give up the hope and enthusiasm we once had and buy into the "this is how this is supposed to be," "this is what you are supposed to do," and "this is what you are supposed to think" mantras. We may at some point decide this is not a mask we will wear—we are done and will no longer accept these beliefs.

If we choose a spouse or significant other who has bought into a belief system similar to those we are removing, he will have us putting that mask back on and adding several more. When our love is fresh, new, and exciting, we want to please and be accepted by the one we choose. We as women want so desperately to love and be loved; we want what the heart wants, sometimes knowing in our heads that this could be a bad choice for a mate.

When we choose a man from a dysfunctional background who has not had counseling and did not do the work necessary to be healed and made whole, we are going down a very difficult and sometimes dangerous path. Only God can change the damaged heart, mind, and soul of a man; we are fooling ourselves to think that we can change him. And what's worse, if he comes from a dysfunctional family, we are also marrying into that. Early in the relationship, he is on his best behavior, trying to gain acceptance and love. Professional marriage counseling is needed before saying "I do" so that we know what we are walking into with our eyes wide open. He may choose to have his family out of his life temporarily to get and keep you, but chances are, in the future, they will be back in his life, and now in yours, which may be a huge burden and point of contention. If one comes from a different socioeconomic background and a more functional family, the two (plus their families) are not like-minded and will clash like light and darkness. It is difficult to deal with people who do not share similar family values and the same standards of acceptable behavior as a family unit.

Choosing an unequal mate will often end in tragedy, such as divorce. It is just a matter of time. In many cases it becomes a hidden tragedy of years of misery played out behind closed doors, which ends like the vows "until death do you two part."

It is unfortunate that so many have died remaining in marriages and relationships that never should have begun (or should have ended as quickly as the revelation that he is not equally yoked to you or he was not one sent by God to you). Many will repeat the cycle of dysfunction when God is not at the center of their relationships. In remarried, newly formed blended family units, both need to agree to get and utilize help to heal and re-negotiate relationships with family members to ensure happy futures together.

If the re-negotiation includes separation from his family members, later there will be blame for the distance between him and his family; arguments will arise and it will be our fault that he is unhappy for whatever reason. As women, we believe love can take care of everything, but we sometimes love so hard, we end up losing ourselves and our connection to God in the process of loving a man who makes life so difficult for us. Look closely at his relationship to his mother—if he is unable to love and truly respect his mother, we cannot expect these men to know how to love and respect who we are as a person, woman, wife, and later mother of their children.

Realize that these men have a heart condition that cannot be healed by our love. Only the love of Jesus Christ can heal these hearts, and we will have much heartache and pain trying to do Christ's job in that man's life. Understand, every woman is measured by comparison to the first woman in a man's life, his mother or grandmother or both. May God help us if he has a "Mommy Dearest." You may be seen as new mommy dearest at some point if he has unresolved mommy issues, becoming the target of his anger and hatred the minute you disappoint or stress him. Those old feelings of abandonment, betrayal, and abuse will surface from past hurts inflicted by his mother or grandmother and erupt all over you. In his mind it is okay to be angry with us but not with his mother, so he transfers all of the past anger or rage towards us and it will spew out, sometimes very violently, for something that most would see as a small issue.

Many times, we are floored, not realizing we have hit an emotional pain trigger with someone until it has occurred a few times. Then we see the cause and effect of a particular word, statement, or action. Once that starts, and they begin looking for things to be angry about or things that they do not like about us; there is no stopping them. It becomes a vicious cycle.

Depending on the reactions they get from us, it may fuel the fire, making them feel better for finally gaining control and being big enough and strong enough to retaliate against things seen as an injustice. They have decided they are done being mistreated, and many times, not making the connection to the past hurts that started this cycle, they are just plain mad in every sense of the word. The main traits and characteristics they say made them fall in love with you are now the very things they say they hate about you. Once this cycle begins, a seemingly endless number of questions come to mind, and we start to worry about all of our decisions—past, present, and future.

It is so difficult not to worry when we are buckling at the knees from the magnitude of issues placed on our shoulders by ourself and others. When we do not set boundaries (or worse, do not clearly state those that we have set), we take on more responsibility, shame, blame, and guilt than is rightfully ours to carry. Broken people do not take responsibility for their part in their becoming broken, nor do they eagerly seek to mend and repair from childhood. Many broken people will not openly admit to being broken, and they wear masks to hide their cracks, gaping holes, and chasms. We cannot control the broken and dysfunctional childhoods and pasts hurts we've endured, but how we cleanse, heal, and repair ourselves for a future as whole adults is fully under our control and is our personal responsibility. We are responsible for teaching others how to treat us.

In so many cases, insecure, delusional, egotistical men do not admit, nor will they fathom, they have a problem, and they will paint their wives as being adulterers or lesbians when they refuse to have sex with them after they treat them so disrespectfully. When we decide to marry someone, no one tells us to look at what we do not like about the man and decide if we can live with those things the rest of our lives. Some of the things we do not like will be there "until death do, we part." In some cases that maybe sooner than we think if the relationship goes to the dark side quickly.

We are shocked many times when we really see the duplicitous personalities, the one shown to the public and the one reserved only for us and close family. Some men are naturally confrontational to a degree, and as soon as they decide they are unhappy, everything they know about pushing our buttons will surface, and it is game on, escalating the confrontation. We become enemy number one. The now back-and-forth plays of love and hate are filled with very calculated chess moves of seduction, manipulation, and dysfunctional behavior centered around sex, money, and control. Once the marriage is reduced to a game of power plays, lies, and schemes, it continues down a slippery slope we are not prepared to endure. At some point in these situations, we will stand in disbelief at what just came from their mouths and actions, even questioning who is standing before us.

Some women unknowingly marry narcissist or psychopaths. We wonder if these character flaws were always there and how could we have missed them, or if this was something new that crept in somehow. I think the best advice we could offer to friends, mothers, sisters, and daughters contemplating serious relationships and marriage for the first time (or again) is to tell them to look at the faults these men have first and decide if they can and want to live with those flaws today and the rest of their lives before they fall in love with their attributes. We can choose to have a life sentence of misery, spend a decade or two of imprisonment, or set ourselves free as soon as possible.

We as women are afraid to be seen as failures in marriage and family, so we put on masks and pretend we are living our dream life instead of admitting the truth about the relationships we're in. Some still buy into the "old maid syndrome," that if we are over 35, this is our last chance at having a husband. We settle for or we stick with the one pursuing us because we do not want to be alone now that we are older. Some are afraid of being judged, especially if we have chosen to marry a man who is wrong for us from the beginning or who becomes wrong and unequally yoked with us later on due to spiritual, personal, or business issues and desires. We are afraid to be judged if we change and grow apart, if we are now contemplating divorce, and especially if it is divorce number two or three and so on. Some couples are unequally yoked, constantly pushing each other's buttons, and are not harmonious together. Their situation is made worse by all the opinions of well-meaning people who are on the outside looking in, who have not experienced similar issues or who are living in misery themselves and like having company. Many do not realize that professional help is needed at times just to get out of the relationships and situations alive. (Some abusers can and will change, but it will take the love and grace of God for it to be a life-long change.) Many have lost their children for years when these narcissist and psychopaths run away with their children and their dysfunctional families help them hid the children. Unfortunately, many of these women cannot afford great help and the tangled web of state-to-state laws. It takes many years to reconcile relationships with their children. The many years of guilt and shame for having lost their children for years can only be healed by God.

And while there are two sides to every story and the truth may lie in the middle, no matter what has been said or done, no one deserves to be disrespected and abused verbally, emotionally, or physically, especially in front of their children. People make comments based on their perspective and what they see as acceptable behavior. Others make careless comments without taking time to fully understand the situation.

It is very hurtful sometimes and further crushes our soul when family and friends make comments that sound and feel like they are criticizing our actions. It may feel like we are being told we have brought the abuse upon ourselves and he is not completely wrong for all he has done to us. So many cannot empathize unless they have walked in the shoes of an abused woman; they cannot imagine how devastating it is to have been delivered and set free from our abuser only to be additionally wounded by the words of those who do not understand. They have never been subjected to abuse on a daily basis at the hands of the one who is supposed to love and protect them.

It would be nice to hear that our family and friends support our decisions, but it is understandable if people decide to stay neutral during a divorce for their sake or that of the kids. Don't get hung up on expecting or needing their support. We also do not need them to agree that the abuse in all its many forms is wrong, no matter what the reasons were. It is understandably hard not to hear our family and friends express any anger towards the injustice of what has been done to us, but it is imperative to forgive everyone in order to focus on priorities and find stability. Yes, it only expends more energy to try to convince others to feel as we do! At these moments, we need to save our fuel to survive and get to the next step in our new life.

Know that you are not alone. You can still claim a new life for yourself, even though you may feel forsaken in the midst of a battle. God is with you. Seek out the support of those who have been in your shoes; they know how it feels to have the lack of support and understanding of some family and friends who have not experienced divorce, depression, and devastation. This is new and confusing for everyone, so forgive and renegotiate relationships and learn to keep your business to yourself.

When relationships change or there is a disconnection, people deal with them differently based on past experiences and how those changes will affect them. In the case of divorce, we forget that other family and friends had their own separate relationship and connection to our spouse and therefore, find it difficult to figure out how to navigate and deal with the divorce from their perspective. There is sometimes a lot of conflict in many different relationships while the entire family figures out the new ground rules or acceptable behaviors before, during, and after a divorce.

Some families need to go in for counseling to deal with the impending divorce or during the divorce. For some close-knit families, the extended family members may need to be included in this family counseling, if they are willing to participate. There are families that struggle for many years because they are in a time warp and are not sure how to deal with the changes, emotional pain, and memories that surface. Divorce issues also shine a light on past hurts and re-open wounds or scars when expectations are not met, such as a lack of support and encouragement. This situation invokes memories and hurts that trigger our cellular memories of past emotional pain.

Unfortunately, the reality is that some family members will not go to or fully participate in counseling due to stigmas and fear of being judged by others. Divorce-related issues that begin in childhood, can continue into adulthood without help for resolution. They go from generation to generation in many families, and no one makes the connections to find the root cause to begin the work of repairing minds, bodies, and souls. In dealing with the matrix of connections past, present, and future to the people, places, and things in our lives, we must go back to our earliest memories. We need to find the root causes of these issues and understand why we have made the decisions we've made and why we have allowed certain people and behaviors to be prevalent in our lives. We also need to learn how to rectify them. We are responsible for our own development, growth, and healing as adults. No matter how old we are, we can embark on a journey of removal and rebuilding in order to gain wholeness of our bodies, minds, and souls.

In speaking to many women of different ages, I have found that we all come to a moment when our hearts and minds become aligned with each other. It is when women say those three words, "I am done." At that moment our minds are not going back and forth between good and bad memories. We are not replaying in some fashion the voices of manipulation in our heads, or coming up with reasons to justify behaviors. At that moment, our hearts are aching from so many wounds. All we want is relief. We're at a point where we are just existing and have become numb due to the constant pain. When that moment arrives and we say, "I am done," our minds and hearts are in alignment and no longer at odds with one another. They agree it is time for a new season.

This alignment signifies a season coming to an end and the preparation for a new season begins. We may have all said, "I am done" before, but in staying and tolerating things we don't want, we lie to ourselves and others. Through the confusion of our lies and the feelings of failure, resentment, and lack of gratification, we become afraid and paralyzed, sinking back into the miserable routine of our self-imposed prisons. We believe, and others believe, that we do not really mean what we say and that it is said only to make a point or to manipulate a person or circumstance. In some cases, because of the stirring up of old feelings of abandonment, worthlessness, and pain, the mere fact that we had the audacity to utter those three words may make the situation much worse. All of our relationships suffer when we and others do not trust our words, integrity, judgment, and gut feelings.

In examining our lives, many of us realize that at different times we are unequally yoked in various relationships, both romantic ones and friendships. There is a time and season for everything, including relationships to change. Although it is sad when people leave our lives, we need to learn to let go of relationships that no longer serve us well. If we keep certain people in our lives, especially up close, many times our growth is stunted because we are unequally yoked to these people. They may try to hold us back if they are fearful of growing or fearful of us outgrowing and abandoning them. As we examine our lives, decisions must be made regarding various relationships and the impact on our future.

At some point, a husband may sense when we are done dealing with him and the issues or abuse in the marriage. He has lost sight of how to rectify the situation and, with all the compromises and tradeoffs made by both, the list of offenses grows. We find ourselves under the rubble of the destruction that occurs when we become more angry, bitter, and lost.

In many cases, both spouses have been wearing numerous masks from years of hiding and being in bondage, playing roles that appear as if we are living our happily-ever-after fairytale that so many women dream of as little girls. He is lost, too, and has also forgotten who he is or would really like to be. When two are joined together, where one goes the other must go as well, so when we awaken, so must he.

The process of awakening and becoming aware may be more than he thinks he can or wants to bear. We fight things that are uncomfortable, even though growth and development are good for us. The process of healing pain actually becomes more difficult with each stage of healing, because the pain intensifies as we bring it to the surface. In creating new truths, behaviors, and habits, time and consistent hard work are required (which is extremely difficult with opposing forces close to you). If we are on a mission to grow and develop, those closest to us need to be on the same journey or we will find that we have outgrown them. It is very difficult and exhausting to go in different directions and on different levels from someone with whom we are closely connected to in life. Just like the process of healing ends with feeling wonderful, in most cases of divorce, the objective is also being pain free and feeling new.

Our kids probably reached the point of being done long before we did, because they love us and don't want to see us suffering over and over again at the hands of someone who is supposed to like and love us. Many times, from the onset, the kids have clearly seen what we refuse to see as bullying and abuse. Kids are very aware of the chaos and confusion in their homes, and they get tired of it quicker than we do. It is amazing how we lose or let go of our awareness at various stages in life, especially when we don't want to see life as it is at that time. Children sometimes see friendship, love, and proper behavior from a clearer perspective than adults. Those six-to-ten-year-old children gain their perspective of relationships from school rules and life on the playground. They know friends are supposed to be nice to each other—bullying is not allowed, and name calling is also going against the rules. These children living in abusive households are confused when they go home and those rules from school and the playground are not followed. What's worse is when they have to live with a bully. When the bully is their role model, especially if the bully is their only role model, it is no wonder so many kids are bullies these days. Due to a lack of whole families getting counseling during and after divorce or loss of a loved one, and with so many kids going from one home to another, kids have anger and resentment that they don't know how to properly handle and heal. Some children become victims at school also, and unconsciously connect to those who will inflict more abuse upon them.

Unfortunately, women often stay in unhealthy relationships because they want their children to have two parents. However, what they are teaching their children with the words and actions of one who stays is that it's okay to put up with disrespect, abuse, addiction, etc. It is so important to be honest with our kids because, in most cases, they know more than we think they do. It is just as important that we listen to them because some kids are so wise and see more clearly than we can at that time. In many of these situations the kids are in danger as the abuser targets the children seeking to inflict more pain and torment or to gain more control. If one parent will not leave or rescue the kids, they may feel unloved, unprotected and unworthy, which follows many into adulthood.

It is not necessary to give our kids all the disturbing details of why our marriage ended, but make sure they know that they are not to blame and that our goal is to create a new peaceful home environment for them and ourselves. Explain new goals and desires in terms they understand, like the rules they have learned about friendship, love, and proper behavior at school on the playground.

New goals and desires for our new life may include dating and remarrying, so make the children aware of that desire to remarry before there is someone new in our life. It is so important that they have time to deal with the possibility that someday we will be remarried. It gives them a chance to express their thoughts and feelings, as well as time for us to do the same.

If more counseling is needed, it is best to address it before the new love of our life shows up. Our children may shed great insight that will help us in choosing or recognizing our new love. As single moms with children, we come as a package deal, and more issues arise when we choose someone before considering how the children and their personalities will mix with this new man (and his children, if he has them). For some of us, the process of getting out of a bad marriage is so consuming, we do not have time to think about how to deal with dating and courting emotionally, mentally, spiritually, and physically. The physical aspect of relationships has required many hours of prayer and counseling, depending on the mode of abuse or dysfunction in the marriage. As if the transition through divorce is not difficult enough, now there is so much more to figure out at this new stage of being single, especially with kids (such as the difference between dating and courting from a spiritual perspective as well as "where does life go from here"). Think about WHY you want someone new. Is it a healthy reason? OR do you feel like you still need rescuing? That's not a good reason. One should feel secure and worthy, etc. without a "new man," and before one shows up.

When we are over 35 years old and dating again, it sometimes feels as though we are in a recycle bin being picked over. We see dating as a means to an end because we are still looking for our fairytale, the happily ever after we always dreamed of having and never got. For so many we feel screwed if our first husband remained a frog in spite of all efforts to turn him into our Prince Charming. It would have been great to have learned about the dangers of being unequally yoked before saying "I do."

But for many, as we awaken, we realize that if some of our choices had been different, we would not be who we were intended to be at this stage in our lives and we would have missed out on some amazing lessons. We would also not have had the children we had, each with their unique characteristics and personalities created purposefully by God. We must make peace within ourselves and see everything is as it should be, good or bad. The time we spend getting through the stages along our journey to where we should be is the issue, so we must decide if we will spend 40 days or 40 years becoming our best selves.

The unraveling of two lives after divorce is very taxing, with very long to-do lists that must be done before dating again. We go from joint accounts to individual ones, name changes on utility bills, beneficiary changes, dividing possessions, and the list goes on and on. Life after divorce and widowhood is what we make it. Just like anything else in life, it is both heaven and hell.

If you were married for many years and did not cheat, there will be some apprehension when it comes to that first date (and probably with the first few dates). We forget that it is only a date; it is in the here and now and is not in itself our future with this new man. Many times, counseling is needed to help us reprogram our thought process regarding dating and platonic friendships with men because we may feel as though we are cheating while on a date. In cases of past abuse, you may not have had male friends due to the jealousy issues of your spouse. Or, sub-consciously, you may have feared that you would compare the differences in these male friends and your spouse and then run for freedom. Yes! Learn how to have healthy friendships with members of the opposite sex.

The first few dates are scary enough without thinking about getting married again and dealing with children, exes, ex-in-laws, family, friends, and how many Christmas dinners you will have to go to now. Counseling is a great place to start to figure out who you are now as you go into the new relationships you are forming with male friends. If you do head down the aisle again, if you are lucky, your future husband will have gone to counseling already, too. It is a great idea to go to marriage counseling and marriage seminars together before saying "I do" for the first time, but especially after multiple times of being married and divorced. We'll discuss more on this later.

We all make mistakes in dating, which is why so many of us have kissed numerous frogs who did not turn into our princes. It is a part of life--the blessing is in learning from those mistakes and putting that knowledge to good use to help ourselves and others. Many of us find that in sharing our stories, we help others and ourselves with these lessons. As stated previously, we have to share our stories with each other in hopes of saving lives, particularly those dealing with any form of abuse. We just need to pray for guidance during dating and try hard not to become or be seen as desperate. Loneliness can cause the most stable person to do crazy, stupid things to get attention from someone of interest. If you spent many years feeling lonely while married, it may be more difficult and confusing when you start dating and get positive attention that you are not accustomed to receiving. It helps to laugh much (and often!) at yourself during this process because you are human and to err is human.

Whoever tells you dating and courting are just like riding a bike, please run away quickly. They do not have a clue about dating and courtship. They may think they do, but pay close attention to who they are dating or who they married before taking their advice. Do not do what you did in the past, expecting different results; you will get what you got if you do what you did.

For those whose Mr. Wonderful is unfortunately deceased, know that you were blessed and could be blessed again, but still proceed with caution. This is a different time and season; use discernment. Some men are looking for a "Sugar Momma" and you will have gotten involved with someone for whom you are not prepared, and then will be floored and financially broke weeks, months, or years later when you ask yourself "Who is this person?" This is a question that so many of us have found ourselves asking when we realized we did not know or like this person that we had married, and wonder when and where it went so very wrong (especially if you had Mr. Right the first time).

Growth and development cause us to look at ourselves, and then to examine those people, places, and things around us. The nuances of divorce are difficult to understand for a spouse who was happily married and their spouse died. Sometimes a widow or widower does not truly understand the intricate web of emotions associated with divorce especially if their new spouse is still dealing with resolution of past trauma and trust issues. Some spouses may struggle to understand when they marry someone who is divorced that they should not invite the ex-spouse to events without agreement. It is imperative to communicate early in relationships and to explain concerns for agreement of who can be invited to an event in your home, as well as verbalizing that your home is your safe haven, especially if the divorce was bad due to abuse in any form. Candid conversations are needed to help those who have not been subjected to abuse or dysfunctional marriages to understand.

It is very important for couples in blended families to discuss and agree upon ex-spouses being invited only to certain major events, especially if the dysfunctional behavior or strife spoils the joyful family gatherings. Big, happy, family gatherings are not joyful for many divorced spouses because they are dealing with a corpse at the gathering—a living one, but a corpse all the same. The ex-spouse may still look like the person they loved and married but not behave like the person they knew when they said "I do", and big extended family events are not the place to deal with unresolved issues.

The widow or widower does not understand this dynamic because their corpse has been buried. Plus, if they were happy, the two relationships are like day and night—they are not dining with their enemy like the divorced partner has to at every family gathering. It is so difficult to have the "Big Happy Family gatherings" if issues are not resolved, and the reality is some issues may never be fully resolved. We all grow, develop, and advance to different stages at different rates, which is why so many opt for several smaller family gatherings instead of including all the exes with all the new spouses. It is a blessing that seasons and stages change with everything, and it takes prayer and divine guidance to find what works best for you and everyone else. It is an amazing sign of great growth for all involved when the "Big Happy Family gathering" is truly joyful for all.

When we are "awake," we come into our own groove and see our own growth and development as the seasons change. Intimacy takes on new meaning at this stage in our lives—physically, mentally, emotionally, spiritually, and financially. One of my 80-year-old widowed friends shared with me thoughts on intimacy from her perspective as a mature woman. In her 20s she was curious about sex; in her 30s she learned enough to enjoy sex and feed her curiosity; in her 40s she was comfortable enough with herself and her skills in and out of bed to ask for whatever, whenever, and however she wanted it; in her 50s she forgot about sex most of the time and intimacy went to a deeper level; in her 60s she decided she was willing and able to pay for whatever she wanted; and in her 70s and 80s, she prayed for intimacy when she thought about it and remembered that it was good, very good. Unfortunately for some, intimacy does not have good memories attached to it. But even with that dysfunctionality, it is never too late to heal and create new, better memories, as well as gain an understanding of godly courting. Dating and courting are about love, laughter, and happy memories. You can begin now to make new happy memories and forgive and forget the deeds of those that did not serve you well.

We need to take into consideration where we are in our emotional, mental, and spiritual growth when we start courting and dating again. Consider when you had your last "first date", as well as when his was. Knowing when his last date occurred (in high school, college, 10 years ago, 2 years ago, or yesterday), helps you to get a feel for his mentality towards courting and dating. We must ask questions to find out whom we are dating and to know what they want from the beginning of this new relationship. Decide what you want and set your boundaries up front. If the answers to the questions are not in alignment with what you have decided you want or if he oversteps your boundaries, cut the ties immediately.

It stands that the "same old dating game" is still being played; the only difference is the players are older. Some of these men become petrified that you are trying to immediately snag them as a husband. If this is the mindset they once had or currently have due to a bad divorce, be careful. We may change our minds about what we want as a relationship progresses, and it is normal for that to occur, especially when we have not consulted God first. We are constantly growing and changing as people. We must be mindful to renegotiate any agreements and relationships with others that no longer work for us. As we grow and change, we see new and old relationships with new eyes and learn to communicate differently, which means that those around must communicate differently with us as well.

Good communication is the key to learning lessons while dating with as few problems as possible. As women, we get our hopes up and sometimes start moving too quickly, even on the first date. We start mentally planning a life with him, and by the time we get out of our own heads, we don't realize our date has run in the opposite direction because he has picked up on those cues. He hasn't even thought about life with us (and definitely hasn't mentioned it!), but we have planned the proposal, wedding, and homelife, so he is off and running, while we stand there wondering what happened.

It is very helpful to talk to male friends who are also back in the dating world. It helps to get a male perspective on courting and dating and to practice simply communicating with a man. Be aware that what starts out as gathering information, learning from your friend, and understanding the differences in how men and women think and communicate, could turn into an attraction due to the comfort level you may have with one another. For some of us, it may be the first conversation in a long while with a man that did not end in an argument, and you are so thrilled that you may be the one who makes a pass at him. We all have different ideas about courting and dating, but it is so important not to bring old patterns and baggage into new relationships. We must also be mindful of being so eager to have companionship due to loneliness that we rush into the first possibility for a relationship that presents itself. Work with a counselor to keep from dragging old characters, baggage, and your ex into your new relationship, and to keep from searching for a specific knight in shining armor. This "knight" could just be a figment of your imagination and not the man that God has for you in this season.

One male friend expressed to me his amazement that women would reveal their vulnerability and desperation as they spoke of their desires for marriage and children. It was scary and overwhelming for him. He was receiving more information than he could digest on a first date. In desperately seeking to find a mate, these women don't understand why he has not called to ask for another date. They cannot see that they have scared the man off with their desperation for their "happily ever after."

Some women have gotten so accustomed to just settling for anything, that if this new man is just a little better than the ex, they think they have hit the jackpot, and surely God in his infinite wisdom placed this prince in their lap. These women start moving quickly out of loneliness and do not consult God about clear set boundaries and desires being in place first. Unfortunately, many women who think they hit the jackpot do not realize that they have once again married the same type of man until the honeymoon stage has ended. Some stay married, thinking, hoping, and praying there will be changes and they will become equally yoked. A friend who is an attorney stated that the majority of the divorces handled in her office were, at the core, based on disagreements and on being unequally yoked regarding sex, money, how to run their households, and how to raise their children.

It is amusing that many times we leave God out of the dating and courtship but want to bring him into the circus of a wedding and messy marriage. This is how we become involved with partners with whom we have no harmony, and as we grow and develop at different rates, we become even more unharmonious. We are truly blessed if we can take an unraveling marriage and put God in the middle and weave it back together like a three-strand cord, making it stronger than ever.

We must be careful who we allow to speak into our life. This discernment should be initiated early in any new relationship, personal or business. It is so important that we keep all exes from controlling our new relationships with manipulation, as well as keeping them at a distance to prevent sabotage of these new relationships. Also, we must listen closely to what is not said. New or old people in our lives will tell us with_their actions who they really are at their core. We must be very mindful of who we are connected to in our personal and business lives to avoid the mistakes of our past.

Our attitude is everything and it dictates our energy, which draws to us everything and everyone. Change your attitude, change your energy, and change your life. Do not settle for being in the continued presence of those unequally yoked to you, or you will find yourself enslaved over and over again.

Are you done being financially broke, broken, controlled, confused, and limited? Only you can decide when enough is enough and when you are ready to transform your worlds physically, mentally, emotionally, spiritually, and financially to transform into who you are called you to Be!

Chapter Five

~The Single Housewife~

"God is not looking for gold vessels or silver vessels. He is looking for willing vessels."

~Kathryn Kuhlman

For your maker is your husband; his name is Yahweh, Commander of Angel Armies! Your Kinsman-Redeemer is the Holy One of Israel! Isaiah 54:5

My first step in transforming my life physically, mentally, emotionally, spiritually, and financially after divorce and numerous setbacks was turning to the Word of God. I needed to figure out who my Creator said that I am. God blessed me by allowing me to reconnect with my childhood friend Sandra Beck Miller who wrote the book *Balancing Blessings and Obtaining Order*. Her book was very helpful at this point on my journey.

I looked at my life and realized I had left God out of many decisions I had made in my 20s and 30s, which is why I was constantly questioning things and struggling with those decisions. I had to reevaluate all relationships by consulting the wise sages why, what, when, where, who, and how. This included my relationship with God.

I previously spoke of forgiveness in regard to forgiving others, but at this point I needed to focus on forgiving myself also. I had chosen and connected to people, expecting them to meet needs that only God could meet for me. I found that the process of forgiving myself and others helped me deal with trust issues and my unrealistically high expectations of others.

In learning who God says I am, forgiveness ushered me into His presence for a closer relationship with Him. This friendship with my Lord and Savior Jesus redefined me and, in getting to know Him, I was able to really know me. It was a process just like any other friendship. The closer I got to Him, the more I longed to be in His presence, to learn more about His character, traits, personality, and roles. He became my everything because He is truly perfect in all His roles. His character and traits do not change like the wind. He is the same yesterday, today, and tomorrow. Because He is always the same, I could trust in Him for everything. He showed me over the years where He was by my side, even during the times I could not see my Friend (who was always there in times of need). In the days of my darkest hours, I finally and fully understood that all I really needed was Him. I was truly set free, delivered from entanglements and the need to please others.

My life and decisions (then and now) seemed crazy to those on the outside looking in, but to Jesus and to me, all was and is as it should be. I found that secluding myself was the only way to keep my peace during dark hours, those times when I knew He would work it all out for my good, but I just wasn't sure what that process entailed.

I had seen visions and others were sent as messengers to confirm what my dear friend Jesus had shown me. I know that my life lessons are not just for me. These lessons and experiences formed my story that is being put in black and white to help others transform and transition into Proverbs 31 women.

My dear friend Jesus became the lifter of my head as His Spirit bestowed gifts upon me such as love, joy, peace, patience, kindness, goodness, gentleness, faithfulness, and self-control. After numerous setbacks it is hard to press forward when your world seems to be coming undone or shattering, especially in the eyes of others. I truly felt like the least of those among whom I connected to in my familial, social, and business circles after dramas and traumas brought me to my lowest point of having very little left. There were many days that I wondered if I would come home and see my dirty laundry spread across my front lawn and the locks changed on my doors, a testimony of my shameful and humiliating downward spiral for all the neighbors and those passing by to see.

I felt most vulnerable and naked when I lost all my properties, especially my home for my sons and me. With every setback I learned just how strong I was as I looked for the lesson and blessing in each. It was not easy to look for blessings in some of the setbacks that hit me hardest. I struggled many years with some issues and traumas. I was embarrassed many times by having become so financially broke and broken. My battle with poverty had started years ago, but the evictions started a visible battle that could be seen by all onlookers. Many times, I felt humiliated and mocked by the comments of others who did not understand my journey and mission that God had for me in this season of my life.

My biggest failures and battles were in relation to money and the lack of it during each passing year after my divorce. When I was stripped down to owning nothing of any substantial value, I became a clean slate for God to rebuild healthier and better than ever. I realized what was important and necessary; was that which could not be bought.

I learned to be at peace and expectantly trust my Lord to protect and provide for me. He had established a track record with me over the years, and as He told me, He would never leave me nor forsake me. No matter how it looked in the natural world, I knew from experience I could count on Him. I understood counting on Him meant sometimes He would send one of His other beloveds to assist me or do something miraculously. My faith and trust grew until I had peace that He would be with me and provide for my needs and desires in the right time, just like the sun rises to provide light at the right time.

In due season I was able to begin readjusting my course in various areas of life. This helped me to see my journey more clearly as the visions began to manifest before my eyes. I was able to finally see things coming into balance and feeling well within my fractured soul before all changes occurred, knowing my course in life was determined long before I was born. In becoming friends, family, and a constant companion with my Creator, I became friends with me, myself, and I. We became one as He fused together every part of my fractured soul.

He led me to His Word. First Corinthians 13 gave me an understanding of His perfect love that allowed me to heal my broken heart and mind as well as evaluate all relationships, including the one with Him, at this juncture of my journey. He then led me to 2 Corinthians 6:14-18 (NIV): "Do not be yoked together with unbelievers. For what do righteous, and wickedness have in common? Or what fellowship can light have with darkness? What harmony is there between Christ and Belial? What does a believer have in common with an unbeliever? What agreement is there between the temple of God and idols? For we are the temple of the living God. As God has said: "I will live with them and walk among them, and I will be their God, and they will be my people." Therefore, come out from them and be separate, says the Lord. Touch no unclean thing, and I will receive you." "I will be Father to you, and you will be my sons and daughters, says the Lord Almighty."

My Maker also became my husband and the lover of my soul; He became my everything. Loneliness was previously my constant companion. Even at times when I was surrounded by others, I did not always feel like I belonged amongst them. I couldn't understand why I felt just as alone among a group of people as I did when I was by myself.

Several of the poems I have written were love letters to the Perfect Prince Jesus, and once I started a love affair with Him, loneliness and unrest disappeared when I was in His presence. I learned to find and pull the pieces of my heart back together to give my whole heart to Him, knowing that my Maker could put all of those broken pieces back together and rebuild it like never before to serve who I am in this season and to love Him more deeply.

My heart healed as I expressed my love for Jesus. My relationship with my Lord was the key to setting me free to authentically be the real me—alone or with others. I was and am being taught how to be Jonquil, the characteristics, traits, personality, and essence of me as I take a closer walk with my Jesus, my everything. My roles and connections were continuously being changed or reestablished, and as my heart healed, I longed to be a wife in a godly marriage with my Lord at the center of it. I found peace in the revelation that He was preparing me and putting me in the right place, for the right man, at the right time.

God had placed or kept me in seclusion off and on for years, and periodically I would feel lonely. But I knew I was not to seek and find anyone in the flesh. I realized I had to stop dating because I was out seeking my new Boaz. But nothing felt right, and I knew in my heart I was out of alignment. I really did not want to make a mistake and choose someone wrong for the evolving new me. God reminded me that His word says, when a man finds a wife not when a wife finds a husband.

I asked the Lord to help me understand dating and courting from His perspective, so He led me to meditating on Isaiah 54:4-5 (TLB): Fear not; you will no longer live in shame. The shame of your youth and the sorrows of widowhood will be remembered no more, for your Creator will be your "husband." The Lord Almighty is his name; he is your Redeemer, the Holy One of Israel, the God of all the earth.

In the process of my Maker becoming my husband, I started reading more on relationships (especially on the topics of love and respect) to better understand my role as a godly wife first with God as He continues to prepare me for my new husband. I had been a wife for 15 years, and for years after the divorce, I struggled with my identity because I still saw myself in the role of wife. I was a wife with no husband, and I struggled greatly in all areas of life while briefly dating after divorce. I did not fully understand the difference between courting and dating. There is nothing more irritating for a single mom than taking the time and money to get our hair and nails done in preparation for a date and make arrangements for our kids, only to have that date cancel at the last minute or be stood up.

Dating after divorce is like a mine field of unknowns, with many little emotional explosions that send you into bouts of depression that send you to bed with the covers over your head while curled up next to a pillow for comfort. I found that in talking to other women over the years, I was not alone in my confusion with my role as a wife in search of a new husband. We never imagine. When we walk down the aisle in joy and splendor as a new bride, we never imagine the sadness and ugliness of becoming a widow or ex-wife.

Some women spend many hours in despair, praying and longing to be made any man's wife again. Some spend years waiting expectantly for God to bless them to be a wife again in a godly marriage with a man who is equally yoked with or to them in a harmonious relationship with Jesus at the center of it. I found the book *Love and Respect* by Dr. Emerson Eggerichs was quite helpful as I meditated on these pearls of wisdom:

> "Lord, I do believe; help my unbelief. I want to follow you, and I want to do this unto you" (see Mark 9:24; Ephesians 6:7-8)."

> "In the Ultimate sense, your marriage has nothing to do with your spouse. It has everything to do with your relationship to Jesus Christ."

As I learned to trust, love, and respect Christ as my Maker and husband, I knew He would work everything out for the best for me. My Perfect Prince is my companion who walks with me through my life missions. He has provided, protected, served, and led, as well as given me great insights, while I walked shoulder to shoulder with Him in friendship. My Lord first loved me, but I was not able to fully receive from Him until I could trust and feel worthy of His unconditional love for me.

In the previous chapter I stated that we too often leave God out of the dating and courting. He is not consulted on many of our relationships from the beginning because we do not first have a close trusting relationship with Christ. If we consult God to determine whom we should marry and God's timing for that marriage, we would lessen our heartaches and pains. Courtship helps us prevent giving our heart away piece by piece in casual dating relationships. Due to so many of us not understanding the difference between dating and courting, we end up fragmented instead of whole when we get married. This is why the divorce rate is so high now as compared to that in the time of our grandparents who understood the purpose of courting. They also did not throw in the towel on their marriages as quickly as some do today. The high divorce rates have added to multiple divorces becoming very prevalent since many do not seek counseling before or after divorce. I found that these women will marry the same type of man again, resulting in the same or similar problems due to never resolving those issues or breaking those soul ties, entanglements or connections from the past. These poor souls find themselves feeling like they are reliving their past over and over again. Single moms today have resources such as support groups, unlike our mothers, who felt ostracized in the culture of that generation if they became single moms. Things change, like the average age in which people marry now, has increased, and casual dating in teenage years is common now. Romantic attachments and entanglements are formed earlier with numerous people, and pieces of one's heart and soul are given away to each partner we have._We profess to love each one with all of our heart and promise to never love another as much as_we love them. We have no clue what we are doing to our worlds and that of others with these emotional ties. But worse are the detrimental sexual entanglements and ties that add much deeper levels of connections when not severed spiritually before marriage.

It is apparent why so many marriages are in trouble when we really look at the difference between dating and courting as well as the depth of connections and types of marriages we enter into or think we have entered into due to ignorance or deception. As we stray away from God, we fall prey to unbiblical practices and principles that eventually bring about confusion and devastation. While dating, many do not set up boundaries or keep those boundaries the longer they date a person, nor do they seek guidance and counsel in the beginning to prevent their attachment to the wrong partner. Some women years later find themselves unmarried with children, living as common law wives with those wrong partners, and some end up married to the wrong partners due to a lack of knowledge and guidance on dating and courting. In receiving guidance and assistance from godly mentors and friends, they might set up social events in an effort to help you comfortably get to know possible suitors for courtship. We can ask questions and get the feedback of our mentors and friends instead of relying on only our wisdom and discernment, because God may show them something that we may not be able to see in ourselves or the other person. It is most important for those of us who were previously in bad marriages to have godly mentors in godly marriages. Through our mentors, God is able to guide and prayerfully prevent us from giving our heart away too soon especially if we have been alone for quite a while. This guidance could also help to prevent us from choosing the same type of man again, just with a different name and face.

In receiving sound guidance and counsel, different types of marriages should be discussed by the parties to determine their needs and heartfelt desires in regards to their mission and walk with God in conjunction with a spouse. Some couples decide to marry solely based on soul and body. Other couples marry based on soul, body, and spirit, meaning they have sought counsel and included God in their relationship. These marriages are first and foremost based on spirit, to bring glory to God by joining the two individuals together as a power couple in God's kingdom. These couples are brought together supernaturally. They do not casually date, but they may know from the beginning because God speaks, letting them know that they are to be married to one another. They court with guidance and are brought together to build the kingdom of God through their combined God-given missions, gifts and talents. These parties court instead of dating so that when they join in holy matrimony they are not fragmented in marriage. The partners in a kingdom marriage have a close relationship with Jesus Christ. This couple has been chosen to serve the kingdom of God foremost, making Him the center of their lives, so each partner is whole and prepared to be joined to one another with God at the center of their union.

When I put Christ at the center of my life, I found peace in realizing that He first chose and loved me, and then I was able to fully receive from Him. I learned that I could trust and rely on Him with each passing day. He let me know that I was special and worthy of His unconditional love. His words of love have readjusted my life's course and transformed every area of my life. Becoming completely bare to expose my foundation required yielding to being broken and stripped down in stages, making me accustomed to being vulnerable and unashamed of my nakedness in the presence of God, as it was in the beginning. My setbacks in life and love became stepping stones to lead me down the path to Him and to the plan that He had for me. This is GOD's Word on the subject: "As soon as Babylon's seventy years are up and not a day before, I'll show up and take care of you as I promised and bring you back home. I know what I'm doing. I have it all planned out—plans to take care of you, not to abandon you, plans to give you the future you hope for. When you call on me, when you come and pray to me, I'll listen. When you come looking for me, you'll find me. Yes, when you get serious about finding me and want it more than anything else, I'll make sure you won't be disappointed." (JEREMIAH 29:11-14 MSG). In yielding to being stripped clean of all I had known before I experienced His Agape Love, His Love replaces the sometimes-tainted experiences of human love, erroneously connected to negative words and acts, such as those I experienced from people from my past. We are lacking the meaning of Love expressed in 1 Corinthians 13. God is Love and He never fails, and if we remember what His word says about Love, we are able to keep our hearts from being torn into pieces. Through ungodly dating and marriage, we sometimes settle as we are desperately seeking to be wife to those who do not know that Love is patient not impatient, kind not cruel, rejoices in the truth not lies, always protects, always trusts, always hopes and always perseveres. Love is also not envious, not boastful, not proud, not rude, not self-seeking, not easily angered, not delighted by evil, and Love does not keep a record of wrongs. To love and be loved is the greatest gift we can give and receive. It is the greatest of missions to serve, by joyfully sharing faith and hope with those all along our journey. I have been taught to focus on my mission and to share my message as I walk out His plan for me as His wife only until he brings the husband created for my later season. He gave me the full name of my new husband in 2010. Everything is not always as it seems or appears to those on the outside looking in, as my future unfolds with my Perfect Prince. Although I am single, I know that I am His housewife, His Proverbs 31 woman. Although to some I appear to be the least of these, but I know that I am valued above rubies and vastly wealthy with things that do not perish. I am His and He is mine as I contently await my man of noble character in the fullness of time, we will become a three-strand cord that is not easily broken.

Chapter Six

~Pennies In My Purse~

"You can only become truly accomplished at something you love. Don't make money your goal. Instead, pursue the things you love doing, and then do them so well that people can't take their eyes off of you."

~Maya Angelou

"But seek first his kingdom and his righteousness, and all these things will be added to you." Matthew 6:33 NASB

Finances and a lack of adequate finances has a way of negatively affecting the mindset of people more than anything, especially single moms who were stay-at-home moms, those who worked only part-time, and entrepreneurs who had hardships before and during divorce or widowhood. It is amazing how people see themselves based on their definition or connection to money. One's self-worth and value are generally tied to their money, because the spirit of money in society today shows those with less to be considered less or the least of these in comparison to those with more money. I found that I felt most vulnerable and fearful when I had to admit or tell someone that I did not have money to pay for some necessities. During the process of my downward spiral financially, I realized a lot about myself in regards to money, my priorities, and my relationship with God. The energy of money and its connections to people, places and things impacted all of my worlds as this spider web of pathways grew into a matrix that helped reshaped me. I learned so much from this matrix of spiderweb-like connections, intrinsically designed pathways, and points of connections to like-minded people with energy and frequencies in alignment to my own. In looking at those on my pathways at various times I could see how we defined ourselves based on how we defined money with regards to our past experiences and our faith in Christ, as well as based on blessings bestowed upon us. I felt like I was stripped bare without having money and things that I needed and wanted, especially during holiday seasons. I learned the difference between wants and needs as I spiraled downward into poverty, shame, and depression after having lived quite comfortably previously.

Over the years I spoke to other brilliant, hardworking and talented women who found themselves__in similar circumstances as mine. We could not understand what was hindering our progress or causing us to go backwards. We found that we would go in circles year after year, not making much progress on our paths, in our missions or on our plans. It is difficult and embarrassing to have to seek help from any and every one to try to prevent homelessness and starvation for our families; it is especially heart wrenching to have to seek help from our kids as we struggle. Our lives become a battlefield with explosions happening in all areas as we learn to pick our battles and release them each to God. I and others have felt like Noah building the Ark on his front lawn, feeling humiliated and mocked because of our actions, or when our mission is misunderstood or simply looks irresponsible and crazy to others in our lives.

Survival instincts take over as a result of being stripped and feeling exposed once financial crisis has reached a certain depth or magnitude. If we can focus on remaining peaceful during our crisis or battles, great revelations spring forth from within us that we did not know were there, and our turning point arrives. Many times, to find or focus on peace, we have to pull away from some people, especially those not at peace within themselves due to their own battles getting the best of them or those who are concerned for us but do not understand our missions. Depending on how strong we are at the time, connecting to the right people during a crisis is crucial. If those we connect to are stronger than we are mentally, emotionally, and spiritually, they will pull us in the same upward direction of their souls' momentum. This is good if they are more positive than we are, pressing forward and upward, but detrimental if they are very negative and moving backwards. Our priorities become clearer as we stand still in silence, blocking out the voices of the outside world. As we clarify our needs and wants, we determine our priorities as we re-brand and re-define ourselves and our priorities.

Sometimes we can hide, but sometimes we cannot. As a result of being stripped, there is nothing to hide behind because every part of us is exposed. Feeling obligated to answer questions about our decisions or our missions can be extremely stressful. Many times, like Noah, we are awaiting the next set of instructions or directions. There are many women who are not strong enough to deal with the years of questioning and mockery, so they give up or give in and go to the grave with their mission, gifts and talents still hidden within them, doing the world a great disservice. Imagine if Noah had given in and followed the crowd, the broad path, or the suggestions of those well-meaning people. If Noah gave in to prevent further humiliation, his mission would have been aborted. We forget that when we give up or give in, following the crowd, we change the trajectory of our life, that of our children and that of others in need of a ride on our Ark. When we choose to stay the course on the long narrow pathway created for us, momentum is created as we flow in harmony, feeling at peace on our route. We must remember there are other lives, missions and destinies connected to ours in the matrix of the world forming interconnected and concentric circles, creating ripples birthed out of our momentum as we propel forward. We forget we are to serve as role models or sometimes pioneers in Ark building for others to follow in the Kingdom of God.

What is your Ark, what does it symbolize, and how many destinies could be connected to it? Some of us have or have had several Arks that we gave up on or gave in to due to humiliation, because they were not understood by others. It is not for some to understand our drive to complete our missions, no matter the cost or duration of time to complete that mission. For those who persevere, the elation of the accomplishment of such an important task cannot be described, especially once your Ark has blessed at least one person. Remember, our Arks are a part of us, our mission, and their significance are only seen by those it was created to bless. As we look back, even before our mission is completed, it is amazing to see the connections to the people, places and things miraculously brought to us to teach and assist us in our tasks as we confidently and diligently press forward, even during seasons of mockery. Psalms 23:5-6 (TLB) "You provide delicious food for me in the presence of my enemies. You have welcomed me as your guest; blessings overflow! Your goodness and unfailing kindness shall be with me all of my life, and afterwards I will live with you forever in your home." There is no sweeter feeling than seeing our rewards handed to us before the eyes of naysayers, unbelievers and mockers. Do not despise small or difficult beginnings as we build our Arks. Everything happens for a reason, even having only pennies in our purses and only fumes in our gas tanks while creating and building our Arks. It becomes a track record of little testimonies of God's overflowing daily blessings provided for us, such as being able to drive on fumes in our gas tank. We become more compassionate after tough times and some humiliation, because during the equipping and preparing for our missions and destinies our hearts and minds change for the better. The equipping and preparing through tough times enable us to assist and spiritually mother others to help them make it through similar situations to those we experienced by sharing our testimonies of supernatural blessings. These shared testimonies become the fuel of child-like faith spoken as declarations for those who realize that God is not a respecter of persons, and he delights in giving all His children the desires of our hearts and minds. Our brain cells are seeds of energy, creating building blocks that become words, thoughts, actions, and stories, greatly affected by what we allow in our hearts and minds to nourish, deplete, or destroy our or another's Ark. By exercising our free will to choose our Ark, pressing forward to the finish line with positive thoughts, words, and actions, we create testimonies to nourish other's seeds of energy.

Financial crises and experiences uncover who we are and force us to reenergize, grow and develop along our journey toward our destiny. Sometimes we find ourselves in an anxiety-ridden environment while on our missions or building our Arks. Depending on the situation, we may feel like perishing on the battlefield or in the wilderness alone before we complete our mission or arrive at our destiny. These seasons of despair drive us to look at any new opportunity that presents itself, especially during re-branding and re-defining ourselves and our capabilities, especially if we become weary of feeling alone. There are times we miss opportunities when distracted and delayed by unproductive busyness and paralyzed by financial struggles, causing bouts of stress related issues, opening doors to depression and cycles of illness. These crises and experiences show us the belief systems and the masks worn by those around us. Financial issues also uncover real connections, and their agendas in our lives; the crisis will reveal if they were sent to help or hinder. It is important to discern whether people are helping or hindering us, and if they are in our life for a reason or a season. Other people can show up as divine connection, teachers, mentors, or guides. As we spiral downward and upward financially, and as our social associations change, we learn to expect changes from people and not to be offended, because God is the only one who is the same yesterday, today and tomorrow. It helps to remember that people are points of connection. Some come into our life as a single point of connection to people, places, things, or information, and then they are gone. Some people come into our life for a season with various points of connections for us and may reappear here and there to reconnect to us and bring new perspectives, lessons and contacts needed in that season. Then there are those who are with us for a lifetime of connections as traveling companions and witnesses to the ups and downs of our Ark's building process; these are the ones who love and support us when we have only pennies in our purses, as well as rejoice with us, when our financial breakthrough arrives. We are never really alone on our journey. There are visible and invisible helpmates who are sent to assist, connect, and cheer for us along the way to our destiny.

Bravery is required to trust God and keep moving forward, regardless of how things look and feel while on our mission. Trust in God happens just like with any friend; it is a process that builds the relationship through good and bad times, and through lack and plenty. No matter how long the journey to our destiny, we need faith to be brave and stand firm, knowing that He has promised to instruct us along the way and provide for all our needs. Every day we can find testimonies that God has provided for others, either in the past or right now, giving us hope for our future as we ask, seek, and knock.

~God's Love Letter to Frightened Women~

Dear Beloved,

I am fully aware of where you have walked. You see, I am the One who has sustained you through all the places of hardness as a good soldier and I brought you forth to this day. I am a God that does not fail in any of my performances for those who put their trust in me. I'll not disappoint them; I'll not put them to shame in their expectations of me. I don't want you to fear man. I don't want you to look to the right or to the left. I don't want you to have your ear open to the counsel of man alone, but I lead you now by my Spirit into my Word; your ear will become more in tune to my voice, I will direct you in the path of my Word. I will enable you to know how you will conduct yourself. My Council, my Spirit will I give you and I will cause you to shine in this troublesome situation. I will be the vindicator of you and I will declare you righteous and I will expose the evil and I will frustrate and defeat your foes. I will tell you now to look up; your help comes from above and it is the help that made the heavens and the earth and there is no need for you to fear man for you can boldly say, "the Lord is my helper and from this day forward you can say that God is for me. He is on my side; He takes my part." Take courage now, I give to you, strength today and I give to you, peace now that passes your understanding and it will amaze you as it reigns in your mind and in your heart. For I will enable your mind now to be stayed upon me that it might be kept in perfect peace as I work to do that which, only I can accomplish, and one day you will see this enemy fully destroyed before your eyes. Just as I told my people to stand still, before I closed the Red Sea, they never saw that enemy again. I am able, I am able, keep that in mind, I am able, says the Lord, to do exceedingly abundantly above what you could even dare ask or think of me.

Just rest now in me and be still and know that I am God, for I shall be exalted above the heathen in this situation, and all will know that you are mine and that I am yours. Do not be fearful confronting those who come against you and do not be fearful concerning those that I have given you as the fruit of your womb. I am able to keep them as I have kept you through all these years and brought you forth to bring glory to me, and I am able to keep them also. Let your heart be at peace now concerning them. I have my eye on them and there is more working for them in their defense; there are the invincible hosts that are in their defense; child, rest in this, rest in this. Know that they are never out of my sight nor are they ever far away from my provision. Let peace now enter your heart concerning them, for I hold them and you in the palm of my hand.

With Everlasting Unconditional Love, Your LORD Jesus Christ.
This is from a passage that was given to me by a wonderful teacher, who taught my son in 2008 in summer school; it had brought her much comfort over the years and especially during her divorce. This passage has traveled the world bringing comfort to all those who receive it. I saw it as a love letter from God, I don't know who God chose as the tool to write it, but bless you for obeying. When I received it, the form was not that of a letter, just in paragraph form, but I saw it as a letter, so I put the words in this format and added what I heard God saying to my heart over the years. I hope it brings comfort to all those who are frightened and in a battle. I also spent much time reading Psalm 91 for comfort, which much of this letter embodies.

Chapter Seven

~Our Search For Significance~

"A woman is like a tea bag; you never know how strong it is until it's in hot water."

~Eleanor Roosevelt

"And so, I say to you: Ask, and you will receive; seek, and you will find; knock, and the door will be opened to anyone who knocks." Luke 11:9 TEV

The gift of faith helps you transcend into your brilliance. Our level of faith can be increased by simply asking for our heart's desire for increased faith. Our levels of faith and trust determine our approach in going before God to ask anything of him. So many women have spent years asking questions in relation to what is their life's purpose and mission, not realizing that the answers were already within them. As women, our desperate search for our significance can only be found when we seek and find our creator and spend time in his presence. We will not find our true significance or importance to the world through the opinions of others, our property, and bank accounts. No matter how noteworthy our career contributions maybe, our transcendence into our brilliance and significance occurs when we find and serve in our God-given area of giftedness and missions.

We are often fearful of being stripped bare, removing our masks, and stepping into our brilliance. We don't know how to deal with being in the spotlight or on stage, having our real voice heard. It can be terrifying for our words, thoughts, intentions, and motives to be in the spotlight or under a microscope, seen and heard by the world. Perfectionism brings about anxiety as we struggle to be seen as "Superwomen", trying to multitask to the tenth power; bringing home the bacon plus having to then fry that bacon and clean the pan, as if that is what makes us significant. Our joy is lost in the desperate attempt for perfection, not understanding that our brilliance lies in our brokenness, imperfections and uniqueness. We have hidden our brilliance in darkness by the numerous masks we have worn for so many years in an attempt to hide our imperfections and true essence. We must then learn to properly handle the questions and attention that is thrust upon us, knowing we do not owe anyone answers or explanations when we step out and let our brilliance shine. According to his word in Isaiah 42, our creator says that we are worthy of being upheld. He says that He delights in us when we choose to serve in the missions, He has given to us, even if that means changes in relationships, our address and our career. He has chosen and equipped us for our missions and destinies as He orchestrates the right connections for us along our journey. These right connections bring glory to him as our mission starts a ripple effect of blessings from the interconnectedness of others' destinies to ours being fulfilled. When we chose and took the first step into our mission believing we too could do the seemingly impossible like walking on water, we develop child-like faith and start fearlessly walking on water, creating those ripples.

Some women are called to pour into others and will not be on the mountaintops shouting their messages, nor are they called out in the streets, traveling across the world with their mission. This does not mean that their significance in God's grand design is less than that of another who is sent across the nation or into the world to make speeches, sharing their message or doing certain works. The ones pouring into others start the ripple effect by interceding, repairing, and imparting into the hearts and minds of the ones called to travel the world; it is the prayers of the obscure hidden in prayer closets building spiritual arks that no one sees. These women, these intercessors, become Godmothers to many, and it does not matter if their new children connected to them in spirit are younger or older, their missions are to mother others by bringing them up spiritually with care, affection, and protection until they are prepared to go into their destiny. God uses these mothers to kindly care for and train his children, who are in many cases seen by the world to be less than and incapable of greatness. These Godmothers are used to show His ability to transform these obscure, lowly women into the great women of God they were destined to be.

These mothers have been given the task to love, protect, repair, and teach God's children who have been damaged and broken in one way or another. This is not to say that our natural mothers were or are not significant in our lives. They, as well as the spiritual mothers, were chosen by God to impart things into our lives. We owe a huge amount of gratitude to our natural mothers for all they have done. We choose who we are from day to day due to what they have imparted into us over the years. God knows that he can trust these spiritual mothers to do what our natural mothers were not capable of doing for us or with us in some cases or circumstances. In the word of God, we are commanded to be salt and light. God knows that His Godmothers understand being salt and light. They will not further bruise nor rub salt in the wounds of his fragile creatures wounded by deception, manipulation, guilt, and shame. They were gifted to be Godmothers to help answer the unanswered questions, help remove masks to lessen their burden, guide them in forgiving those who have disappointed them, and so much more. These servants of God know their significance lies in mothering as they impart light into the lives of their spiritual children. The light of these Godmothers illuminates the way until the flickering lights of_God's children who were once seen as "least likely to succeed" lights have become burning_flames. Once their light is strong enough, they illuminate and light their own paths as he intended, throughout their homes, communities or the world.

Extraordinary women are connected to one another to bring justice to others and to encourage one another along their paths in all areas of life. While prayerfully meditating and thinking about Godmothers who came into my life through divine orchestration one day, the revelation came, and I believe the brilliance of our sun pales in comparison to the illumination of the collective spirits of women connected on a mission for Jesus Christ. I am in awe of my spiritual mothers and how God used them to equip and prepare me by telling me their testimonies of faith. During the unfolding of these chapters I used their testimonies as declarations to build and elevate my faith, enabling me to share my own walking on water experiences on these pages to uplift others.

We forget that while journeying in search of our significance, God promises to be with us and sends those who did not give birth to us to mother, equip and guide us when we need edifying and uplifting. When we have decided that enough is simply enough and we allow our secret_struggles to be exposed, we clearly see the root of our significance. As we stand naked in the spotlight out on center stage to be used by God to bless his other children physically, mentally, emotionally, spiritually and financially we walk in our significance. In the word of God, he also promised to take us by the hand and keep us in perfect peace. He will make us an Ark, a safe haven or covenant for people to whom he connects us along our journey as we are asking, seeking and knocking. We are a light to open the eyes of those who are blind and unable to see the answers in front of them, unable to see the masks they are wearing, and unable to see the solutions to their problems and disappointments. These remarkable mothers to many are used to set the captives free and equip them to go out and set others free from invisible chains and prisons without bars. We are connected to bring light and blessings to dark places and bring freedom to the broke and broken hearted.

The world places such importance on money and finances, using it as a measuring stick of one's importance. Money is the god of many in this world and those with a significant amount of money, according to that measuring stick, are praised like gods. Knowing who we are and whose we are will prevent us from feeling insignificant based on a financial evaluation that does not determine true wealth or shine light on the true provider of wealth. Money is needed in this world, but it cannot buy true love, joy, peace, or health; these are given by grace and kept through deliverance and healing. The measuring stick should be based on the evaluation and validation from God, the one who gives us power to create wealth. Our measure of significance will continue to go up and down if we are looking to others and the world for our significance. If we are looking for validation and significance from the wrong people, those who produce bad fruit and those with whom we are not equally yoked that evaluation will surely bring us down. Those who lack peace who struggle and spiral downward during seasons of lack desire company in their misery. After God has affirmed, restored, and healed us, making known to us how special we are to him, our measure of significance goes up and stays up based on our relationship and favor with God, not based on money and the evaluation of others.

When we desire peace along our journey, we will find it as we stand still and wait on divine guidance. It is imperative we stop doing things that get in the way of our seeking and finding, the unknown that can only be revealed by God to those who seek first His kingdom. We desire certain dreams to be fulfilled because God placed that desire in our hearts, due to the plan that he has for us, to show our significance to him and His importance in our lives. When we are with the right people, in the right place and at the right time, we are informed of blessings that are on the way, bringing newness into the lives of God's people. As newness comes in with those sent to teach and repair us, know that our words, our songs, our thoughts, and actions will all change accordingly, to match that of our mentors. Our mindsets change as we seek to find our significance, while we walk with others on collective and personal missions. Many spiritual mothers also serve as Midwives to help others give birth to their messages and missions by showing us our blind spots, as well as pointing out our relevance to the world and the kingdom of God.

Rejoicing in our souls takes place as we accomplish goals and utilize our gifts and talents to share blessings with the world in books, songs, paintings and more. We are led throughout our search by our mentors as the voice and hands of God during dark times on unknown or unfamiliar paths. God promises to help us, and even though he seems silent, know that he is there listening and waiting until the right time to bring His promised answers, without fail. His light breaks through our darkness, and his divine guidance takes the rough places on and around us and makes them smooth. We are never alone on our journey. Sometimes new spiritual mothers are given the assignment to join us on the next part of our path to re-teach us during times of disobedience. These God mothers are used to help prune us and to impart new teachings needed for new stages of growth, development and to reassure us in new stages of nakedness. These teachings keep us prepared, equip us as we are subjected to shame and humiliation if we fall short on our tasks, and show us how we must turn a blind eye to the mockery of others as we seek, until we find and accomplish our missions and destiny.

During the times that we fail to learn certain lessons, God patiently continues to send teachers in various forms, each using their stories, gifts, and talents to help us finally pass the test, showing that we have learned the lessons for this stage of development. As we progress, we will then start to knock at the door of teachers and sages in search of more wisdom, knowledge and understanding. We are then instructed to listen and look closely, for He is eager to save us from our own ignorance, deafness, and blindness. When we do not honor His teachings, we end up bound, entangled and derailing or delaying what was ours as a birth right. For example, if our father has promised us a car, but if we don't learn to drive and prepare for the exams to get our license, we delay the promised car.

During stages of ignorance, we are sometimes deaf and blind. If we don't clearly hear and see the Lord's guidance, the result is often a downward spiral. People may seem to turn their backs to us during times of hardship, but it is important that we learn to not be offended by placing our expectations on God, not on people. Many times, we have spoken our hardship into existence, and yet we are blind and deaf to what we said and did without understanding our actions. We wonder how people we trust rob, enslave, or turn their backs to us. We may sink so low that there is no one left to come to our rescue because unless someone has walked in our shoes or on this narrow pathway, they do not know how to reach and rescue us. Instead of turning directly toward the Lord when we first struggle, it takes us some time to realize he is all we have left and all we needed in the first place. After our inner man has become so weak, after a lengthy battle with powers, principalities, as well as the inner battle with me, myself, and I, we desperately seek out and finally turn to God for His strength to rescue and revive us. There is nothing like hitting rock bottom and being at war with ourselves and others to turn our hearts toward God and His teachings. We are many times oblivious to what is truly happening around us, blind and deaf to the higher teachings that are beyond our current stage of understanding. It is imperative in this season, as we search for our significance, that we learn everything we can from our spiritual mothers, mentors, and angelic hosts. All the lessons and blessings they have acquired are shared with us to help us live in wholeness and wellness. God intended that we live in service of his kingdom, using our gifts and talents during the stages of asking, seeking, and knocking. God intended that we live with our teachers, walking with us, encouraging and guiding us until we know who we are and whose we are on a daily basis. We are connected during seasons of learning to function in our missions, our purposes, and our significance in the body of Christ to help others to awaken and end vicious cycles that repeat over and over.

T HE LORD IS MY SHEPHERD [TO FEED, TO GUIDE AND TO SHIELD ME] I SHALL NOT WANT.

Psalm 23:1 AMP

Chapter Eight

~Awake~

"History, despite its wrenching pain, cannot be unlived, but if faced with courage, need not be lived again."

~Maya Angelou

Rise up in splendor and be radiant, for your light has dawned, and Yahweh's glory now streams from you! Isaiah 60:1

My wake-up calls came in the form of questions being asked and answered, the removal of masks, the decision that I have had enough, being sick and tired of roles I no longer wanted to play, the learning to trust that pennies and fumes would indeed be used by God to increase faith and that by asking, seeking and knocking, significance would be revealed. We are the sum total of our experiences like my journey from 10 properties to 10 bags in a homeless shelter. Everything in our journey is used by God; nothing is wasted, even seemingly unimportant chance encounters can unexpectedly be used as a story that blesses someone more than we realize. God knew the magnitude it would have at the right time with the right person. With Jesus, we can redeem the beautiful memories that have been long forgotten or tarnished by doors being unknowingly opened to darkness. My wake-up calls also came from divine connections that helped me to learn how to deal with my history, unpack my baggage, unlock chains and doors, withstand the stripping process so that I would be seen in my nakedness unabashed. As doors and windows opened, I was given opportunities to see, hear, feel, smell and taste things that were not of the physical world. These things encourage me to walk in childlike faith and have increased hope knowing that God loves me deeply and wants to connect and commune with me through these wake-up calls.

Awake

The stories that I will tell are my experiences or encounters that I only whispered one on one to some people, as if they were dirty secrets, when actually they involved the supernatural and extraordinary that should be our ordinary as children of God and spoken without embarrassment. Those secret or forgotten experiences and encounters are hidden keys which must be remembered and found. These hidden keys unlock doors within us to rooms harboring spiritual things or strongholds not dealt with due to our lack of awareness. Once these doors are unlocked, we find ourselves at the threshold of strongholds ready for deliverance and healing.

We have to look back or go back to course correct from where we got derailed. We have all had times when we were trying to find our way to a certain destination and we became confused by our Global Positioning System or God's Positioning System, our GPS which may not have updates regarding new roadblocks or detours. Sometimes these detours take us off the well-travelled paths and place us on unfamiliar new routes where we have divine connections and new experiences as we yield to accept the unexpected surprises along our way. If it were not for some roadblocks or detours, we would not have stumbled upon some people, places or things that were needed to teach and prepare us for the next part of our journey. These detours are opportunities to find freedom from strongholds and traumas, and we connect with people sent to help us heal. We also learn to rest peacefully in the delays and detours. These roadblocks sometimes slow us down to see an opportunity to help others. I have amazing encounters that took place during delays, roadblocks or detours along my journey to some destinations or in the midst of my own deliverance and healing process. These encounters are the catalyst for my walking in healing and being set free. At times we tell ourselves that supernatural encounters did not happen because surely it is impossible for that to have occurred. But all we have to do is truly believe what we read in the bible, because God is the same yesterday, today and tomorrow. There are times when we know that something happened but we do not know how to explain it to others, but if we search the scriptures and ask Holy Spirit, we get the words for the explanation.

Nothing is impossible with Jesus. He is redeeming certain memories to redefine them as a way to go back and help us course correct, then move us forward to become who we were meant to be, according to his purposes, and to plan a destiny for us that was preordained from the beginning. As we stop sleeping or sleepwalking and awake to all that God has for us, we are renewed and walk in newness. I pray my stories bring to your remembrance things that you have forgotten; I pray that you are encouraged to tell your secrets that have kept you bound by strongholds; I also pray that your curiosity is ignited to seek out more intimacy with God so that you will go in and out of your Father's house, the Heavenly Realms that are within and about you. I find it amazing how we can all see the same thing, but each have a different perspective and memory of that thing or situation. It is important to write down dreams, visions, and experiences to help you remember them. We all have our own truth based on how we see, hear, and feel both naturally and spiritually. We are all triggered, transformed, and transported through and by different means, for our individual testimony and journey, resulting in us being fearfully and wonderfully made daily by God.

My Roses and Silver Tray Experiences

My fondest memories of my grandfathers are seeing how they served my grandmothers. The simple acts of service they performed were like dance steps to an old familiar tune that he had practiced so often they had become as automatic as breathing but deliberately done daily or often as a gesture from the heart. It is amazing how certain sights, smells, sounds and tastes will transport us back to memories of the past. One day I purchased Rose scented soap and lotion that transported me to the past with the first use of these products, as I look back reminiscently remembering the lovely variety of rose bushes in my grandparent's yard. My paternal grandfather planted, pruned, and cultivated rose bushes and other flowers, not because he loved them but because my grandmother loved them. She had been diagnosed with diabetes when she was younger and he did not want the thorns on the roses to prick her, so he handled them for her. When visiting them for the holidays or summer, we would sit on the front porch looking at her lovely flowers. My grandmother's hair was very long when I was young, I would brush her hair while we admired her beautiful flowers with few words passing between us. Some days we would swing or rock back and forth on the front porch, just watching the dance of the butterflies, dragonflies and bees going from flower to flower. His concern for her well-being reminds me of how Jesus protects us from being pricked or stung by things that would deceive us by their lovely appearance.

As my grandmother set her dining room table, the beauty and simplicity of a few roses in a glass vase or jar in the center of the table, surrounded by her blue and white dishes, exuded loving care and acts of service one to another that spoke volumes without a word. While visiting with them, I noticed that as the roses began to wilt, my grandfather would head outside to cut fresh blooms. I remember following him outside one day, watching how he went from bush to bush looking for just the right roses to cut and de-thorn before bringing them into the house. I also remember him teaching me to catch dragonflies and bees in jars to observe them closely for a little while, then release them to dance from flower to flower once again. The flowers added simple beauty and magnetic color that drew my eyes as the sweet scent of roses wafted through the room, before food was placed on the table and its own scent overpowered the delicate smell of the flowers. The smell and sight of the roses bring reminiscent visions from my childhood of their table-setting of blue and white dishes surrounding by a few thoughtfully chosen beautiful roses.

During vacations, I was back and forth from my paternal grandparents' home to the home of my maternal grandparents, since they lived in the same town in south Louisiana. My maternal grandfather had always made coffee in the very early morning hours, and one morning on my way to their bathroom, I noticed him bringing a small silver tray into the bedroom. As I watched, he served my grandmother her cup of coffee while she sat in their big high bed that looked giant to me. My grandfather was well over 6 feet tall, and my grandmother was petite, maybe 4'10 at her tallest. I am petite like her, and my grandfather was always a gentle giant in my eyes. The next morning, I got up when I heard him stirring around in the kitchen, I went to the bathroom and when I came out, he saw me, picked me up, and placed me in their big bed next to my grandmother, Mama Dear as we called her. He went back into the kitchen and returned minutes later with the silver tray with a cup and saucer of coffee for my grandma and a tiny demitasse cup and saucer of milk with a splash of coffee for me, since I was maybe 5 years old. As the smell of coffee filled their room, I felt like a princess sitting next to my grandmother, the queen, on their big high four-post bed that both my grandma and I had to use a step stool to climb on to. There is no better feeling than being gently lifted to a place of warmth and comfort and lovingly served by a king. That sweet gesture of my grandfather serving me coffee on a silver tray showed me that the fairy tale was real for me. I was his princess. I was royalty and worthy of being served, like the stories that were read to me.

As an adult I started "sleep walking" and forgot how I was served coffee in bed during those visits. I forgot that I was a princess and was supposed to be treated like a princess because I was worthy to be served. I did not make the connection until I started writing these experiences and remembering that, after he died from stomach cancer when I was 10 years old, the comforting smell of coffee became the stench of death and the sweet taste of the royal treatment became bitterness on my tongue, not knowing how to process the painful sting of death called cancer. When he was hospitalized, I begged my aunts to take me to see him, but kids were not allowed on that floor. However, both of my aunts were thick ladies and had worn full skirts, so one held out her skirt in front of me and the other held her skirt out in back of me and, since I was below their waists I was concealed by skirts and was able to walk between them to go spend time with my Papa. As we headed to his room, my aunt told me that my great-grandfather, the father of my paternal grandfather, was in the room we were passing on our way to their father's room. I walked into his room to see him and say hello since I did not remember him. It had been years since he last saw me. He was in his 90s, and he thought that I was his daughter since she and I resemble one another. He was a gentle giant as well, similar in stature to my other grandfather, being well over 6 feet tall, but he had long white braids, one hanging over each shoulder, laying on his chest. He reminded me of the Native American man that I saw on a commercial who had a tear that streamed down his cheek while looking at litter defiling the natural beauty of the landscape before him. As I stood by his bed, he could not speak much, but he called me his daughter's nickname and my aunt told him who I was. As he held my hand and looked at me, his eyes spoke volumes. As the energy passed from his big hand to my very small one, there was a connection that I do not have words to describe, other than to call it a transference of unspoken words or something. I left his room and headed to the room of my king who had lovingly served me coffee. I later found out that he served all seven of his daughters coffee in their beds over the years. I think that may have been the last visit before the loss of my soft-spoken gentle giant, Papa. I was not allowed to attend the funeral, but I stayed with my paternal grandparents whose house was down the street from the church where his funeral was held. I saw the procession of cars that seemed to be miles long as they crept by, like a stream of sadness that was palatable for me. It was like hot bitter black coffee that was once warm brown and sweet, served with love.

Following my Papa's example, I also planted, pruned, and cultivated rose bushes and other flowers in the yards of my first two homes. I enjoyed gardening and I loved watching my flowers grow and bloom, especially in the garden of my first house, where my flowers were exceptionally beautiful. Sometimes I would cut flowers and bring them inside to enjoy the beauty and scent. In my second house the yard was small, and the rose bushes were of concern when my sons were outside playing, so they were cut down to prevent my boys from being pricked by thorns. I just realized that I did not bother to plant any flowers at my third house, the one I lost to foreclosure that I spoke of in previous chapters. I had a huge yard and my sons were older, but I did not plant flowers, only herbs in pots that did not seem to grow very well. After a while I no longer made time to work on any of my hobbies that previously brought me joy, like cultivating roses. Those memories of simple acts of service and love were buried beneath dust, like perennial flowers that died back or were cut down in winter and did not return to grow and bloom in the spring. The magical fairy tale memories of real-life experiences of my kings cutting roses and catching dragonflies in jars, and of coffee being served on silver trays as I perched on a giant bed, had been long buried under dust beside my memory of what it feels like to be a princess.

I believe that everything is redeemable with Jesus, especially memories of feeling like a princess with my Papas, so I sought to uncover and reconnect my memories to positive emotions and beliefs. I went to my friend and Pastor who has a coffee house and told him about my silver tray experience to help me redeem my memory of coffee with my maternal grandparents. I asked him to help me redeem that memory by serving me a small cup of coffee. As I sipped the coffee, I remembered how it felt with them, recapturing the comforting smell and the warm brown and sweet taste of the royal treatment. As I wear the scent of rose lotion or smell fresh roses and wear my dragonfly or butterfly necklaces, I fondly think of my paternal grandparents, and I have decided I will plant, prune, and cultivate roses again soon. As my happy memories were redeemed, I saw the connection between my years of digestive issues and these memories buried within me that had become disjointed, disconnected, and distorted by the devourer, cancer. However, Jesus Christ paid in full for our victory over everything, and it is His pleasure to redeem roses and silver tray experiences as an act of service, a simple gesture from His heart. All that is needed is for us to Ask, because all things are possible with Him!

My Phillip and Things That Go Bump During The Day Experience

Previously I mentioned that on my 40th Birthday, while at a women's fellowship, Sister Barbara asked me about the spiritual things that I only discussed with my maternal grandmother. I told her that I had asked God to take away the gift or ability to see in the spirit realm years ago. I told her, she was the first person that I had discussed this with in many years, because it frightened some people and some people saw me as weird. I also told her that some people tried to debate with me regarding theology and the validity of the need for deliverance now, as well as other supernatural things mentioned in Bible. After talking with Sister Barbara, I gained clarity later that night, and I asked God to let me see spiritually again, because now in my maturity I am able to discern and handle how others perceive this gift or ability. Some people may still be frightened, some people may still see me as weird, and some may still try to debate, but I have learned over the years to let go and let God deal with those things. It is not my business what others think of me or how they perceive what I believe, see, and hear that is between them and The Lord. In reading the books and teachings of others, I have learned to look at teachings like a buffet and simply partake of that which engages and delights me now. I have learned to leave the rest of the information or teachings until later. There are times when I will go back for more when my body and soul are ready to digest and assimilate more information. Some of these experiences in this chapter are a result of what transpired in the months and years after my conversation with Sister Barbara that night. My encounter with her was my birthday present, the catalyst to my asking God to open my eyes and ears again to see and hear all that He desired to show me.

Months after that women's fellowship, I met a neighbor as I walked down the street to tell my children to come home, when I knocked on the door, I was invited inside and started chit-chatting with her as the children continued to play. She was very pleasant, but I noticed there was something awkward that transpired in the conversation, so I told the kids it was time to leave. Days later we all reconnected as the kids played together again. I noticed again the drooping of her eyes as we conversed, and I asked what was wrong. She told me that she had narcolepsy. She happened to be unemployed at the time, and I was self-employed, so we started having tea together at her house or mine and thus developed a friendship. The more time I spent in their home, the more I realized some things did not feel right. One day she ran up the stairs, then ran back down the stairs quickly, which seemed very odd. I also noticed a heaviness in their house, and it was somewhat dark, even though the window blinds were opened. I also noticed that sometimes my younger son did not like playing inside their house. They both enjoyed playing outside, however.

She was very technologically savvy, so one day I started praying and asking God for help. God had called me to start a women's ministry, but not wanting to use that word, I called it a networking group. Little did I realize that when I asked God to give back all of the gifts and abilities that he had for me, my connection with her would be truly eye opening to say the least. I believe it began with my laying hands on her and praying for her eyes. Then her narcolepsy was gone, as well as what I thought was dark brown shadow around her eyes. On another day I prayed in her house and then noticed the appearance of heavy haze or soot in the air in her office and family room dissipated. She helped me learn computer skills and to create my new business logo. The more we met, and the more we prayed together, the more peaceful she seemed and the brighter the rooms in her house appeared. Then she started asking more spiritual questions and sharing stories of things that had taken place in this house and her houses in the past.

She went upstairs again to retrieve a book from a bookshelf, and I asked why she runs up and down the stairs. I remember that she ran up and down the stairs the last time. Other than those two occasions, she did not run. She told me that she does not like to go upstairs and certainly not stay upstairs. I told her I didn't not understand that, since her children sleep upstairs. If she was frightened of something upstairs, she as the mom should be protecting her kids. So, I told her that we are going to pray upstairs, but she told me not to pray up there. I grabbed her hand and led her upstairs, not taking no for an answer.

As we reached the second floor, I saw what looked like soot and a light red smeared bloody hand and maybe paw prints on the walls. I looked at that mess and told her after we finished praying, we would clean the walls as if what I had just seen was normal. As we reached the top of the stairs and I looked around, surveying the space and number of rooms, I asked her which room we should pray in first. I felt led to head into to her oldest son's room first, but she said no, let's go in my youngest child's room. Once again, I grabbed her hand and led her inside the oldest boy's room. I felt something, and smelled a horrible stench that was not normal human body odor, but as we stood in the middle of the room, I was not sure what the feeling or the smell was that attacked my senses. She told me that her son had been pummeled by things he could not see during the night, and he was sometimes bruised. She also told me the music that he plays sometimes while lifting weights sounds like devil worship. I looked on his dresser and noticed that what I saw in the photos concerned me, since it looked like the faces of his friends were morphing as I looked at them. So, I grabbed her hand and we hit our knees to pray for her kids. As soon as I started praying, I felt things were running around us. I heard growling as I held her hand, and I felt it tighten on mine. I told her not to move because this is her house, and she needs to reclaim her home and drive out whatever is harming her kids. After I said that, I was pushed by something behind me that I did not see but knew something was indeed there. I started praying more intensely and asked God to send in a legion of Angels to put a hedge of protection around us as two mothers praying for children who are ignorant to the deceptions of the enemy. I then heard marching, like the cadence of many soldiers marching, similar to what I grew up hearing when my dad was stationed at an Air Base. I looked up, and coming through the wall was golden light in the game-room. Then I felt a large presence come in the room and stand behind us and I could see a veiled image of a very large angel. The atmosphere of the room changed, and the stench was replaced by a sweet smell that I can only describe as the smell of flowers and sugar cookies.

I then felt led to go into the game room where I had just seen and heard the sound of soldiers marching and saw the light coming through the walls. As I entered the gameroom, I looked at her and said, "I did not know you had a media room". When we came up the stairs, I saw a wall there, not an entrance to another room. She told me they do not go into that room any more since her daughter and her friends did something in there with one of those demonic boards. So, I grabbed her hand again and we headed in there, as I told her we have angels here to protect and help us take back possession of her house and kick out everything that is not of God. Her husband came home, and I asked him to open the attic so that we could bless and anoint their entire house. As we went inside the attic, she and I stood at the entrance of the opening, praying, and her husband stood on the ladder below us, holding on to both of us. I asked if they saw the dark hooded beings that I saw crouched down in all of the corners of their attic and they confirmed that they saw them, and their gold eyes also. I know some might think we were delusional, but we were not sharing a group hallucination. A few days later she decided to call her Priest to come and pray through the house also, since the hooded demons did not leave. I told the young Hispanic Priest that he needed to go up into the attic, because that is where the issue was, and as he went up the ladder, I could tell from the size of his eyes and his body shaking as he descended that he saw them also. He asked me where did I learn about these spiritual matters, and I told him God and Angels told me what to do. He left, visibly shaken, after quickly descending from the attic!

Over the next few weeks, we had various spiritual experiences together as I continued to pray with them in their home. I also started praying more in my home, and then I heard growling sounds on the outside of my walls, so I went out and anointed with oil the entire perimeter of my home and property. I prayed that my property would be covered with the blood of Jesus from the very edge of the front of my property to the edge of the back of my property. I prayed the blood of Jesus would cover my property from the edge of the left side to the right side of the property. I also prayed that the blood of Jesus would cover my house from the top of my chimney to the bottom of my slab and every square inch inside and outside. After doing so I noticed that if someone's spirit was not good, they could not comfortably stand on my property, and they would step into the street. There was a guy that started jogging in the street every time he got near my property, but as soon as he passed my house, he would get back on the sidewalk. I noticed it happening often, so I continued to pray that the blood of Jesus would be spread over my entire house and property, and that anything and anyone not in alignment with Jesus would be driven off or away from my property. After seeing and hearing all of the demonic things in my neighbor's house, I decided to cover my own home.

One evening after going on a walk together, my neighbor and I stood talking. We looked up and the sky had a beautiful pink to red ring that seemed to encircle our area. That was truly breathtaking. There was what appeared to be a cloud shaped like a dove. As we stood looking up at the sky, it started getting dark. There was something amazing about how the stars and planets appeared that night that seemed unique in comparison to all the other nights. I looked up, fascinated by the night sky. But this newfound night sky fascination was different than the ones I had after my astronomy class in college years ago. I started praying and thanking God for the beautiful display of his glory in the sky that night. Then I clearly heard it is now time for you to go home and get inside before my wind blows, so I told her something is about to happen. I was just told by God to hurry home. As soon as I closed and locked my door, the wind blew fiercely through our neighborhood. After that night there were days when I looked up at the sky and it looked like Angels fighting in the clouds with swords drawn awaiting or engaging an opponent.

Awake

One Saturday morning I got a call from her oldest son begging me to come over because they needed help with their mom, since things were worse than ever in their house. As he spoke to me, I heard in the background a voice that I did not recognize saying, "no not her" and growling. I must also tell you that they did not have dogs of any size to make these deep loud guttural growling sounds. I prayed and asked God what should I do, and I was told to go to their house. My older son was at an orchestra performance, so I took my two younger sons and put them in my bedroom and put snacks and drinks in the room and turned on the TV and instructed them not to leave my room until I came home. I had on my yellow robe, pjs and slippers with anointing oil in one pocket and holy water in the other as I grabbed my keys to drive down the street, since it was cold. When I arrived, her three kids were sitting outside on the front porch wrapped in blankets with petrified looks on their faces. I anointed them, then went inside to assess the situation as foul voices, sounds and smells of things I could not see greeted me at the door. The children all started talking, giving me the run-down of what was happening during the night and morning that led up to what I was about to encounter in their parents' room. As I went into their room, my friend was on her bed, but her eyes went from a strange black emptiness to her normal eyes, and as they shifted back and forth, she whispered, "help me please," then many other louder voices spoke to me. Her husband was sitting at the foot of their bed in his underwear looking dazed, confused, and petrified as well, so I anointed him with oil as I did the kids and started praying and praising Jesus.

I remembered that a few months earlier a friend had told me about a church to which she thought I should connect. At that time, she mentioned that she heard the Holy Spirit say the Pastor had a message for me. He did in fact have a prophetic message for me, so I started attending, believing that God had connected me to them to learn something special. Now while praying in my friend's home, I was told by Holy Spirit to call that same pastor. It took several hours for them to arrive at the house since their GPS was not working properly. While awaiting their arrival, I was sitting on their bed, hugging both of them as I prayed for them. Her husband went to go check on their kids after he left, I felt a peaceful presence next to me, so I said, "I know you are here to protect me, please tell me your name," and I clearly heard "My name is Phillip." I could faintly see him as light instead of a shadow. I had sensed the presence of Phillip in the past, and had seen his image over the years, but I had not thought to ask his name until I was looking face to face or eye to eye with dark forces. When the Pastor finally arrived with his wife and one of the church deacons, he asked me why I had come into this situation alone, warning me of the dangers at hand dealing with such activity. I told him that I did not come in alone, that God told me to come here when I asked him what to do, and that my Angel, Phillip, was with me. They took over and I watched and listened and continued to praise Jesus and to thank him for setting the friend I loved free from the legion of darkness. After a while without going through all the gory details of foaming from her mouth and other issues, she was free of many of the demons that had earlier identified themselves as Legion. Their kids asked to sleep over at my house, and I let them so that they could get a good night of peaceful sleep. The Pastor asked them to come to the church the next day, so I fed them breakfast then sent the kids home to get ready for church and had all of them follow me in their car to the church in order to receive instruction on what to do to prevent this from happening again. Simply put, the instructions were based on Matthew 12:43-45 regarding how to keep their house swept clean so that the spirits would not come back with friends, becoming seven times more. In Matthew 12:43-45 "When a demon is cast out of a person, it roams around a dry region, looking for a place to rest, but never finds it. Then it says, 'I'll return to the house I moved out of,' and so it goes back, only to find that the house is vacant, warm, and ready for it to move back in. So, it goes looking for seven other demons more evil than itself, and they all enter together to live there." That Sunday afternoon I cooked dinner for their family at my house. Once it was getting close to bedtime, I noticed they did not want to leave, but I knew if I did not send them all home, I would have a whole family living with me and my sons. They needed to courageously take control of their house according to the instructions they received and occupy it confidently.

As the weeks went on, I started noticing her saying negative things about the Pastor and his teachings in comparison with her beliefs and thoughts. I also noticed that the atmosphere of their home seemed to get dark again. So, I prayed and asked God what was happening. I was told to look at her eyes closely. I did, and I could see the darkness around her eyes returning. That same week I saw them sitting on the side of the street in the next neighborhood that we pass through taking our children to school. I stopped and asked if there was an issue with their car, and they said no, but as I looked intently at her eyes, I saw darkness and I asked the Holy Spirit what he would like me to do. I was told to go home and not go or allow my kids to enter their house again. I told my kids what I had been told by God and reminded them of the things that had transpired there, because it was becoming seven times worse than before. It saddened me to see that she was choosing to reopen the doors to the darkness that took work and sacrifice to close, so I called the Pastor and told him what I saw and what God had just told me. He explained to me that she had had spiritual issues since she was young, and that it was a difficult battle for the entire family, and it was about choosing to follow Jesus like never before by addressing limiting beliefs and thoughts that would keep them bound. The strongholds of her family were generational and deeply entrenched. I realize now that my neighbors needed mental and physical deliverance and it would take hard work that they seemed unwilling and unprepared to endure, since deliverance is a layer-by-layer process that needed to be embraced as a family for complete freedom for the household. This was a battle for their worlds mentally, physically, emotionally, spiritually, and financially. Many people are deceived, even after they go through such an ordeal, believing that things that go bump during the day and night are simply figments of imagination, and then they allow the squatters (demons) to come back in as they pretend darkness does not exist!

Bertha's Transmutation and Blue Eyes Shining Experience

In a previous chapter I mentioned that my sons and I named my van Bertha, so one day as I was driving, I was distracted by some issue that was bothering me, and I did not see that the turning arrow had changed to red. I looked up, and three lanes of cars were coming towards my van. It was as if everything slowed down and I felt someone pull my hands from the steering wheel and push them to my lap and pull my feet and legs back from the pedals. I saw that the other cars seemed to pass right through my van as if Bertha were a vapor and not solid. There was an odd peaceful calm feeling that I had as I watched my van go through the intersection through all 3 vehicles in the 3 lanes and come to a stop. My van came to a stop in the right-hand lane just past the intersection and I clearly heard, "you can drive now." I noticed that my van was still in drive as I sat in that spot for a moment while I processed what had just happened. I thanked the Angel, probably Phillip, for saving me and then proceeded to drive to my destination, in awe that Bertha and I supernaturally changed in form, or transmuted.

My encounters with Heavenly beings have been as simple and lovely as a message of encouragement as well as protection and lifesaving supernatural feats. I have been blessed greatly by these divine encounters that were sometimes visible, and sometimes invisible - only heard or physically felt - that have blessed me greatly. On several occasions, during very trying times, I have seen Angels that looked like grey-haired older grandfathers that each said the same thing to me, "Just keep smiling young lady, everything will be okay," they would typically say it more than once, then walk away and disappear. They all had brilliant youthful blue eyes that did not seem to go with the grey or white hair and winkled faces. Their amazing eyes seemed to shine through me and bless my heart as they smiled at me.

One day an older black gentleman in an electric company van rang my doorbell and asked me if there was anyone who could help me to prevent my electricity from being disconnected. I told him I was not sure whom to call and he told me, "You should call your sister and I will wait with you while the bill is paid over the phone." After my sister paid my bill, he told me that God was not upset with me, and that God loved me so much and needed me to know that he was not upset with me due to my divorce. The gentleman had spoken details that he could not have known if it were not for God telling him. He also had grey hair and shinning brilliant blue eyes that gently soothed my heart with peace and reassurance, telling me that I was the apple of God's eye. I thanked him for being so kind to me and we said goodbye. I looked out my window as I wondered if God had just sent another messenger Angel to me, the man and the van disappeared, I thanked God for sending this Angel.

Manifested Dreams and the Chasing Rainbows Experience

I have always been a dreamer at night and during the day. Some of my dreams have taken months or years to manifest, but some manifest within days. I had a dream around the time of my birthday, and in this dream, I saw myself crossing over a vast chasm. There was dry parched land where I was standing. I stepped across the chasm onto steps carved out of the dirt and rock. These few steps led to a platform near lush green land. As I climbed the few steps to reach the platform, a man in a white robe was standing next to a small table cutting and preparing to serve cake to another woman and me. He handed me a piece of cake on a saucer and said, "Sweets for the sweet," I was excited about the celebration and for having crossed over from the dry parched land into lush new green land. Later, while with a friend at a Faith Conference, I realized she was the other woman in my dream, celebrating and eating cake with me. We had met 10 or 11 years ago, and our situations were similar as divorced moms. As I drove us to the conference, I started telling her about my experiences with The Courts of Heaven. As I listened to the Pastor speak, I realized that she was the one in my dream, and at the end of the conference I told her about this dream. The next day she asked me to share with another lady the information that I had shared with her about The Courts of Heaven. Days later she told me she briefly shared the Courts of Heaven information with another lady from out of state, who then asked if we would come visit and share this information.

I wanted to make sure that I was going where God would have me to go, so I told God that I needed a confirmation that I was supposed to travel and share this information. I asked him to use my Pastor's wife to confirm my going. Before I could finish voicing it, she started speaking, confirming that I was indeed supposed to go, and that because God had blessed me to be self-employed, I was able to go at a moment's notice. So, after church I went home, packed for the trip and prepared some notes to share with the ladies.

The next morning, I picked up my friend and we set out on our journey as we listened to a CD called "Peace," by Bob and Kim Hazlett, that included various bible verses about peace throughout the music. It was a blessing to listen and pray as we drove through three states: Texas, Oklahoma and Missouri, praising God for what he would do on this mission. This was the first time that God had sent me out of state for a purpose or mission that ended up being about more than sharing information and experiences. When we were about two hours from our destination, we saw the most vivid, bright rainbow that I had ever seen, and we started praising God and thanking him for his promises. Then I noticed that the ground on both sides of the highway resembled the steps in the dirt and rock from my dream, and the land was lusher and greener than where we started the journey. We then saw a double rainbow, and became so excited about what God was doing for both of us in this adventure. I told her after this mission we must celebrate with cake. After the rainbows were gone, we looked up and realized we were now four hours from our destination. We stopped to get something to eat and regroup, as she called the ladies who were awaiting our arrival. As we drove in the dark through unfamiliar territory, we started seeing buildings and signs with the words "grace" and "mercy" on them, as well as what appeared to be, close to the road, cardboard cutouts of Jesus with red and white light shining from his heart. I noticed that as soon as I felt scared, either I would see the cutout of Jesus, or she would see it and tell me it was there, or we would point out "grace" and "mercy".

While driving and praying I heard the Holy Spirit mention Kansas, so I told my friend that I do not know when, how, or why, but we may end up in Kansas. Not realizing that Kansas City is on the border of Kansas and Missouri, we did end up in Kansas City, Kansas and Kansas City, Missouri. While driving, I had seen a sign with $76 lit up in red, so I told her I think we will get a hotel for that amount. We arrived at our destination and started sharing information and experiences. At some point, our host removed her hearing aids and exclaimed that she could hear us and bowed down on the floor praising Jesus. After we had done whatever God needed us to do there, we left and headed to a hotel, having traveled for about fifteen hours due to detours chasing rainbows. We had spotted a hotel near our next destination, so we drove there and got room keys but when I opened the door, it looked like someone was in the bed under the covers. The room stunk of drugs. I gently closed the door, and we ran back to the front desk praying we did not awaken whoever it was in that room. The front desk clerk apologized, then started calling around to find us an available room near this location. It was $76, like I saw on the sign in red flashing lights. I was totally amused by all the signs and symbols that God was showing us as he softly spoke.

My GPS was not properly leading us to the hotel. I did a U-turn and then the lights of a police SUV pulled up behind us. My friend said, "Oh no, you are about to get a ticket" and I said, "No I will not get a ticket, because you Lord sent us here, I did not ask for this. You orchestrated this, so take care of this for me." The officer came over to my window and stated that in Missouri I cannot do a U-turn and that he noticed my Texas plates, so he asked "Why are you here in this area so late?" I told him we were there on a mission for God to do ministry, my GPS was not working, and we had been traveling for over fifteen hours. He smiled and used a flashlight to show me where to turn since there was road construction in that area and it was very dark. We thanked him, then started driving but I passed where he told me to turn, so he pulled up beside us and stated that he would lead us to the hotel. I thanked him and told him that I was close to tears from confusion and exhaustion. He led us to the hotel and told us to park in the empty space right in front that was waiting for us. We thanked him again then proceeded to park in the space just a few feet away. She and I looked at each other as we pulled in the space both thinking as she asked, "Was he an Angel?" We both turned to see the SUV go up the road from the lower little valley area in which the hotel was located and we saw no taillights. In that moment He and the SUV was gone. He was beautiful, with dark hair, a beautiful smile, and yes, he too had shining brilliant blue eyes that seemed to glow. Even though it was very dark out, each time he spoke to us there seemed to be a spotlight above him radiating towards us as we looked at him. We went to our room and prayed and praised God for all he had done and then peacefully slept, eager to see what the next day would bring.

The next day was lovely - a broken heart was healed, and mourning turned into joy when we shared with another lady. She was a divine connection for me since we were both entrepreneurs at heart. She told me that there had been almost 20 murders in that area in the last 72 hours so I knew to pray that peace would come in that area. We prayed at a prayer room, then went to lunch before heading back across the states, praising and thanking God for the mission and journey. After arriving back home I realized that I did not fully understand everything that transpired on that trip, but there was a knowing that we were being obedient and willing to be used, however God chose to use us. I saw my dreams manifested in the physical world as we chased rainbows with grace and mercy. It was a wonderful birthday present to be of use for God, remembering that he is the God of the small and big things, and I enjoyed my birthday cake the following day, knowing that I had indeed crossed over into lush green land.

My Simple Obedience Experience

There are days when I struggle with obedience to God, when it is as simple as giving a message to someone. Sometimes I wonder if it is from my heart or mind or really from God. But when I remember that I am in Jesus and He is in the father, I remember that our hearts are connected, so I give the message and trust that it will bless that person. It is easier to be obedient when God tells me to do something, when it does not directly involve anyone else knowing that God has given me an assignment or message.

I have struggled with obedience to lay hands on people, especially men. I was in church years ago and I heard, "go lay hands on that guy's eyes," and I told the Lord, "But I do not know him." So, I sat in my seat, and the guy remained in his seat several seats down and across the aisle from me. I heard once more that I should go lay hands on his eyes, and once again, I said, "I don't know him." Then I remembered that the previous two weeks I did not know the young woman behind me who had severe burns from her chin to upper chest. She was wearing a scarf and I was told to turn around just in time to see her scarf fall down. As the scarf fell it revealed her black crusty oozing burned skin. I felt an impression that the burns were from having hot wax poured on her, so I asked if I could lay hands on her and pray. I laid hands on her without hesitation or concern that I did not know her, and I prayed for her asking that she would have new baby skin without any scars to remember this abusive incident of hot wax being purposely pour on her to cause harm. Then I gave her the message that her abuser was being removed from her place and that she would not see him again. She came back the following Sunday and opened her top to show me that she had new baby skin without a single scar. She also told me that her abuser was gone when she arrived home after I prayed for her. We thanked and praised God together for her healing and freedom. So, after this celebration came to my mind, I said, "If he remains sitting there, then I will go over to him and pray." I sat for a few minutes, then looked over at him and he smiled but did not move. So, I got up and walked over to the man and I asked if I could lay hands on his eyes and pray for him. He told me that God had told him to sit and just wait for me to come over and pray for his eyes. I smiled, knowing that God was working on me and my discomfort and distrust of men whom I did not know. So, I introduced myself and started praying for this blue-eyed black man from New Orleans, who had already lost sight in one eye, and had blurred vision in the other eye due to a fall. I did not see him again, so I am not sure what happened with his eyesight, I just trusted and thanked God for using him to bless me regarding this new fear of men. It is amazing how God will interconnect and use things to help several people at once. I learned that simple obedience brings peace and makes the experience so smooth for everyone involved. God is able to use us more when we are simply obedient and quick do what we are told, joyfully being of service as one part of the body of Christ. As we ready ourselves to be of use, we are able to, without hesitation or concern, walk in childlike faith, doing what we are told knowing that we are in sales and God is management. As we pray until something happens, like fibroids passing from a uterus, making surgery unnecessary, tumors falling off, open wounds healing quickly, and amputees getting new flesh-and-bone limbs from Heaven instead of plastic and metal, we can believe that God is capable of anything today as in the past, like raising the dead.

God blessed me with a one-bedroom apartment complex for 26 months, and I believe God sent me on prayer walks there as a way to bless my neighbors. Some days I was told by the Holy Spirit to pray that the hearts of the people there would be turned towards Jesus. Some days I prayed for the people that I saw who looked so sad or laden with grief. I also prayed for those I heard crying through the walls. Some days I walked and pleaded the blood of Jesus over the entire complex or the entire neighborhood that surrounded the apartment complex, asking for God's protection from accidental issues with fire or anything that would bring hardship. After 16 months, there was an incident there in the complex. As I sat watching TV, I heard a couple of loud noises that sounded like gun shots, so I looked at the TV to see if someone was shooting, and since they were not, I thought maybe I heard a neighbor's TV. A few minutes later a SWAT Policeman was at my door banging on it, telling me to evacuate the building. I ran out in socks, and he told me to calm down and go get shoes, then follow him. I ran back in and put on shoes, a jacket, and got my purse, not knowing how long we would be out of our building. I was just about to take a bath but had decided to watch some TV first. I thank God I was not in the bathtub when this began. Once downstairs with the rest of the tenants on my side of the building, I was told that a tenant and his new roommate got into an argument and the new guy shot his friend. The officer led us to the complex club house, out of the line of gun fire. As we passed my neighbor's car, my neighbor asked the officer if we could just get in her car and drive to the parking lot of the club house. That is what we did since it looked like the club house would be very crowded due to several buildings being evacuated because of proximity to the apartment where the shooter was located. As we sat in the car, we heard over 100 shots fired between the shooter and the police. It was like being in the middle of a movie as I watched the police run in between the buildings with their big guns. I continued to pray as I watched what I could from my neighbor's car, and listened for updates that were being texted to her from someone connected to an officer. By the early morning hours, it was sad and unfortunate that two innocent men had died because of an argument. It truly was a blessing from God that after well over 100 shots were fired, that there were no other deaths or injuries that occurred, nor was there damage done to any of the tenants' vehicles that would have caused financial hardship to some who were already having a difficult time. Many of the pajama-clad tenants, frightened by the sound of blazing gunshots around the place they called home had looks of horror on their faces as they evacuated. I noticed several moving trucks within the next two weeks as some moved, no longer feeling safe there in the complex. I remained there an additional 10 months, feeling sad on my prayer walks seeing the ribbons that were tied to most trees in honor and remembrance of the two who died. This unfortunate incident started due to conflict after one person kindly invited his friend into his home to keep him from being homeless and out in the cold. I prayed for the families who lost loved ones and would never fully understand exactly what happened in that apartment. Lives_were lost due to premature death through demonic oppression and possession. There was far more going on there during that incident than what most people saw with their natural eyes.

That shooting incident made me miss my house and the season of the tangible presence of God and the Angels outside my front door, the glow and energy of the Angel inside by my entry way and the wind of the Holy Spirit blowing through my house on most days. In my house I felt the presence of God so strongly, and I longed for that as I sat in the apartment, sometimes feeling like the energy of others and their noise was too close for comfort, especially after the shooting. I was connected to God and I could hear Him clearly in my house and in this apartment, but there was a tangible difference in the energy and frequency there in that one-bedroom apartment. I knew that I had to patiently endure and be thankful for this place God had led me to, until He chose to lead me back home awakened, restored and renewed.

I am in awe of his restoring love for me, that he would create Angels that would be my companions, taking care of me and helping me with assignments from God. I am in awe that I can be a friend to God, that he would listen to me talk about anything, and he would answer mundane and sometimes odd questions like which shoes should I wear, and "Which of my shoes do you like, Lord?". I was in a women's conference the first time I heard someone say that He answers and even enjoys it when we include him in the simple things of life just like we would talk to any friend. We were told to ask God how He preferred our hair, and He said, "I like your hair curly, because I gave you those curls." It was such a blessing to hear him say that, and I made peace with my curls, freeing me to enjoy the versatility of my natural hair to simply let it go, wildly curly or straight. He is indeed the God of the small and big things and delights in us as any parent or loved one would; we are indeed His beloved and have a knowing of the depth of His love when we become wide awake. As we arise and shine, walking with our eyes wide open in His glorious light, experiencing things on Earth as in Heaven, our faith, and trust increases. These experiences build our hope and we come to anticipate and expect his promises to manifest His prophetic words.

Awakening shows us who we really are in God's eyes. As we become more awake, we are restored to who God created us to be before we fell asleep as we commenced to sleepwalk through life. We have moments of clarity in the midst of sleep walking, but without continued connection with God, we do not see clearly and cannot understand the sum total of the experiences that mold us into who we are destined to become. As our minds are renewed and we get into alignment with our body, soul and spirit, we are able to observe our experiences as pieces of the puzzle that form the picture of our journey and lives. I have found that through connectivity with God, I have won the battles both seen and unseen, because of his love and protection.

1 Corinthians 13:13 (AMP)

13 And now there remain: faith [abiding trust in God and His promises], hope [confident expectation of eternal salvation], love [unselfish love for others growing out of God's love for me], these three [the choicest graces]; but the greatest of these is love.

Chapter Nine

~The Homeless Real Estate Broker~

"God-given dreams of destiny and success will empower us to conquer our mistakes and nightmares of the past."

~Barbie Breathitt

I gave you land on which you had not labored and cities that you had not built. You are now living in the land I gave you. You are eating grapes from vines that others planted and olives from trees planted by the people who lived there before you. Joshua 24:13 TPT

Jesus is love; He is the lover of our souls. He is always the answer to every question and the light to our paths in every season. I had to know with all my heart He is good and faithful in this season of my journey while searching and questioning the circumstance that had unfolded in every area of my life. Whether our journey is straight and easy, twisty and unpredictable, or dark and frightening, we need Jesus to light our path and guide us. Walking things out in faith is tough to say the least. Especially when we can't see where we are going. It takes great courage to keep moving forward, not in spite of our situation, but because of our situation. The tougher it is to do something; I have found that I was blessed with the strength to push to accomplish or keep moving forward. I have found through my journey and from watching others that something amazing happens after that accomplishment or step of faith. The amazing thing is the pressing forward to achieve, it's not always for us directly, but indirectly. When we look at lessons learned for ourselves and others, we see where the great value lies. The lessons and testimonial blessings are worth more than gold. Those pearls of wisdom are priceless tools we gather on our journey, to be shared with the people who cross our paths, those who are ready and willing to receive them.

In my seasons of harvesting wisdom and tools, I've met amazing mentors, or Titus, women as mentioned in the Bible. Titus 2:3-5 *[3] And here's what I want you to teach the older women: Be respectful. Steer clear of gossip or drinking too much so that you can teach what is good [4] to young women. Be a positive example, showing them what it is to love their husbands and children, and teaching them to [5] control themselves in every way and to be pure. Train them to manage the household, to be kind, and to be submissive to their husbands, all of which honor the word of God.* These verses spoke volumes to me as I learned from the older women who crossed my path. They were divine connections with divine impartations of priceless information to help guide me. They shared their stories, assisting in my growth, and taught me how to share in a way that would assist in the growth of others.

I learned to be ready to receive that which I needed for my next stage of growth. God saw to it that I was not going to be taken advantage of or have to compromise by answering yes to questions to which I should have answered no. It was not God's intention that I compromise in_order to receive those tools of wisdom that were intended for me at the right time in the right place. We all know with certainty that with some people we have to hear the questions then listen closely during and after the question to discern the intent before we answer. But when we ask God to surround us and connect us to the right people, we can answer yes to the questions. Because we know we are destined to receive everything that was preordained for us, sometimes_coming in the form of information, which is a blessing to us and others. Our job is to say yes and have faith He will work out all the details in our favor according to the word of God. Deep rooted traditions or traditional thinking can be thrown to the wind if we stand on His word.

As I accepted and gained revelation that this chapter had already been written for me and that I was destined to walk out this experience as a part of my metamorphosis, a peace arose within me that has remained even when my world was rocked and shaken from time to time. I learned that I had to guard my heart and my mind to hold on to my peace. The Holy Spirit reminded me that it is easy to walk in the fruit of the spirit when I am all alone, but I should develop and grow that fruit with others. When living with others or in apartments, you are drawn in, like it or not, to the dramas of others with their family, friends, and significant others, and they are drawn into your issues, as well. Being in the homes of others or small spaces with little insulation makes it very difficult when you are desperately seeking peace in order to deal with their negative energy and frequency. This influx may invade your presence with discourse, violence, and sometimes crime that can bring a feeling of powerlessness if moving is not an option. Some places or assignments were difficult when my hosts felt justified in treating me rudely, because I was in their home, and they were tolerating my presence and giving me the privilege of not being out in the street. There were times when my heart was wounded by yet another person whom I thought loved or at least somewhat cared for me as a friend. It reminded me of when my son Ryan was about eight years old, and he explained to me that real friends do not bully you or speak mean things to or about you. He reminded me of the rules on the playground so that I would understand who was a good friend with whom to play and who was not a good friend. God truly speaks through everyone and anyone who will help you get the message that he intends for you. He spoke volumes through my son so that my eyes were opened to see that which I was ignoring. I contemplated leaving to get away from the mean-spirited behavior of those hosts, but I was concerned with my safety as well as being in the scorching heat or freezing cold. So, I humbled myself to endure the suffering of the tongue lashings, and I learned to forgive and glean from it something useful. I learned to be grateful to God for the opportunity to gain understanding of His word; out of the heart the mouth speaks, so that I could see the hurting heart of the one giving me the tongue lashing. It didn't hurt any less, and I felt very lonely and weary dealing with the drama of others, not having a place of my own to which to escape, as an emotional safe haven. Sometimes, I would focus on the task at hand as instructed by God and I handled them with grace and immediately prayed for them when instructed to do so by God. But sometimes I did not want to pray for them or deal with them and purposely watched their schedules to determine when to come and go in order to avoid interaction, or I would stay gone until they were asleep.

My Giants will Fall Experience

During one such tongue lashing the Holy Spirit told me to be quiet as I tried to verbally defend my position, because the battle was not mine. I learned that we do indeed reap the words and discourse we sow upon others. I sat quietly as my host stood near towering over me, which is easy to do since I am maybe 5'2." I endured more than an hour of lashings; hearing everything this person thought of me, my faults, and my circumstances. I felt smaller and less significant with every lash sent my way. As I watched and discerned, there was darkness attached to the host who was attacking me. I saw clearly it was not a battle against flesh and blood but principalities. I was able to observe as I sat quietly listening and watching my host as well as listening to what the Holy Spirit was saying to and showing me. Afterwards I was dismissed like a child, so I went to the room I was renting and quietly wept sad tears, like a child that had been beaten but didn't know why. As I spoke to God about those heartless words, that hurt deeply, like salt poured in the fresh wounds of losing my houses, my business, my job, and my apartment, plus my sons in a way, as I had no choice but to send them to live with their father due to my homelessness. As days went by, I avoided this person by seeking the comfort and safety of church services at any church that had evening and midnight prayer services. Later that week my host reaped unfair treatment at work and the event caused hardship to unfold, and that same week she wept before me like a child who had been beaten and didn't know why. She then asked me to pray for her regarding her situation. At first, I silently protested with the Holy Spirit, but I was reminded I agreed to serve in my assignment, to lay hands on her and pray for her deliverance and the healing of her heart. She was wounded from generational curses and a history of being towered over and treated sternly. Throughout my stay, my eyes were truly opened to see the power of words, as well as the power of being driven to the safety of the arms of Jesus and house of God. I was also asked to pray again days later, because she was now aware of a dark presence in her house because she was there all day. My eyes were opened once again to understand how doors were opened by the power of negative words spoken by someone and the intentions of their heart. I saw more clearly the spiritual world connections in her life, past and present, as scales dropped from my eyes to see and understand deeper the word of God. As the Holy Spirit spoke to me in this place and guided me in my assignment here to free a captive who had no idea she was held captive by invisible chains. As I stood, she sat before me and as I laid my hands on her to obediently pray for her deliverance from darkness, I heard the Holy Spirit say, "Giants will fall."

I have stated previously that we have to learn to renegotiate relationships with ourselves and with others as we transform and transition. Previously I also stated that it takes great courage to be truly transparent in the physical world.

Transparency brings us into the spotlight or helps us see that we have been stripped bare. In my stages of nakedness, I had to learn to trust like a caterpillar in motion crawling across the ground looking for guidance, because I could not see much ahead of me due to my lowly perspective. As I crawled at times in my various stages of nakedness, I prayed for protection to keep me from being unduly trampled upon by those who placed themselves above me. As I crawled from place to place, there were times when I forgot my mission was to learn from the experiences that were here to help me continue my metamorphosis. During the seasons of transition and transformation, deeply rooted thoughts and traditions were shaken, broken, then peeled away. Nothing could continue as it had before because everything had been shaken like an earthquake, causing my foundation and walls to crack and break, bringing everything down to rubble. Having no walls to call my own in a season of homelessness, I found things I thought I had lost, as well as acquired new things physically, mentally, emotionally, spiritually, and financially to aid in my transformation.

Connections were made to people, places and things needed for that new season or chapter. It was very humbling and yet empowering learning to hold on to my dignity, knowing the thoughts and the perspectives of others regarding homelessness did not define me or determine my worth or worthiness! I was blessed and highly favored in spite of how it looked to some people. I was so grateful for the grace and mercy that I received, being blessed to not have to spend the nights in my car when I had one. There are some who define homelessness as sleeping in one's car or out in the elements if we do not have a car, rather than sleeping in shelters. Some people do not define having a place to sleep or stay temporarily as someone being homeless. But if the place is owned or leased by someone else, we are always at the mercy of our host and we rely on the kindness of our hosts while in their homes. Sometimes we feel as though we are constantly walking on eggshells or even land mines if our host has never been in our position. We also feel uneasy around unhappy hosts, not knowing what our fate may be in the next moment, and especially when we inadvertently cause the bad mood by hitting an emotional trigger.

In regard to ownership verses stewardship, my perspective changed greatly after spending so many months in the homes of others. After years of owning several rental properties and then having everything removed, I now believe that everything belongs to my Abba Father, and as His child I feel blessed to steward the things created by my father in Heaven. My journey through homelessness has also given me an opportunity to understand the perspective of others regarding ownership verses stewardship. Some regard the ownership of the home that they grew up in as their home forever, so I have found that these individuals never feel homeless. But for those who grew up moving from place to place, there is no childhood home to which one could go back to, and the same goes for those whose childhood home was demolished or sold. For those individuals, that connection to a childhood home does not exist, so when they lose the home that they owned or were purchasing or leasing, they feel homeless. My perspective and understanding changed as I realized that because I had mortgages on the house we lived in and on all of the investment properties, my deeply rooted thoughts of my American Dream were shaken by the realization that what I thought was mine was gone so quickly. That dream was broken as I lost properties one by one until I was homeless. In hindsight I know that I did not make the right decisions and move quickly enough to bring stability to my situation or change my perspective of stewardship. I also see that I allowed shame and guilt to paralyze me in my decision-making process, as I felt my value and worth was connected to those properties and based on my situation, not knowing how to separate my life, my character and essence from my current situation. I sent my sons to their father's house, which was also their home, and I am so thankful that they had another home to go to so that they did not have to endure homelessness.

I am grateful for the peace I gained along the way in the midst of this lonely winter season. I was in search of something, but I was not sure what I desperately desired. I later realized I was hungry for the right spiritual food to build and grow my spiritual world. Through growing discernment, I learned to refuse to eat some spiritual food that was sometimes given to me, because it was tainted. I knew it would not serve me well along my journey and would weaken me instead of strengthening me. My discernment increased quickly during this long winter season; that increase in discernment was imperative for my survival and stability. I learned what and who would weaken or strengthen me. In some of the places I slept, it helped lessen at times the discomfort I felt from the constant warring mentally, emotionally, and spiritually. I spent a lot of time being overwhelmed by fear, doubt, loneliness, and worthlessness until I prayed and listened for wisdom in my assignment for each place. I believe I was on assignment in several places of temporary employment and several places where I temporarily slept. During these assignments my enlightenment and intuition sprang forth and I explored unknown or mysterious things about myself, others and the invisible world of the spirit realms. Connectivity with the spiritual world gives new meaning to life and many times changes perceptions of faith. The substance of things yet seen from the spirit realm turns our worlds topsy-turvy as our spiritual eyes are opened wide.

The temporary jobs were used to teach me things and to connect me to people who needed help, such as freeing some people who had become stuck or stagnant in good jobs that did not make their hearts sing. Some people needed to be freed from working with abusive managers or business owners in bad jobs. Some needed to be encouraged to move them forward along their path to their destiny jobs they were created to do. Sometimes things are "good", but not "God". I was connected to various people from all walks of life and religions. I was connected to various ministries and ministers in various capacities so that I might watch, listen, and learn things of the spiritual realm as well as share what I had learned about the connections from Heaven to Earth and Earth to Heaven. I also learned what not to do and what grieved the heart of God. Some in ministry made assumptions and judged others harshly. Some Leaders spoke out condemning behaviors of others that they themselves were also doing in front of me. My heart was heavy seeing the behavior of some in ministry doing more sinning Monday through Saturday than those in the world, then preaching on Sunday. I was puzzled by seeing in some cases these same sinning ministers being used in a mighty way. I inquired of God to get a better understanding of gifts being given without repentance of sins and why that vessel or person was allowed or permitted to behave in such a manner and then preach to others. I did not want to grieve the heart of God, so I ran from ministry service and from church titles. I find church titles too weighty to live up to especially after seeing the behaviors of some clergy up close and personal.

As I reconnected, I started praying for and laying hands on the sick and casting out spirits once again. I was also used to give messages from God to some of my hosts and employers with whom I stayed, as well as with others who crossed my path. Some of my hosts were not aware that I was there to be a blessing to them. Some of my hosts and employers simply saw me as a lowly homeless woman and made assumptions and disregarded things of which I had knowledge because they focused on my circumstances, the visible things or connections, and not the invisible connections. Some of my employers did the same after I shared my testimony with them. They chose to judge, seeing me in a lesser position and treated me with less respect after hearing my story. Some assumed that I was desperate after hearing my testimony and assumed that they could take advantage of my situation and treat me badly. My trust in God gave me the courage to stand firm on what I would and would not allow, especially knowing that I was there on assignment from The Lord of lords and King of kings and knowing that I am the child of that King. I learned to only share my testimony with those who would be encouraged after hearing my story, and I walked in authority and dominion, speaking freely, making demands and giving commands as the child of that King who is in control of all things. I learned to be obedient and do what I was assigned to do and pray accordingly as the Holy Spirit guided me along the way. I believe my prayers were answered for the deliverance, healing and blessing everywhere I stayed and worked. I stated in a previous chapter how I saw God move in amazing ways as He answered my prayers, many very quickly.

There were some things I understood and some things that were still a mystery to me, as some relationships unraveled and changed, eventually bringing about restoration or renewal as I forgave and let go to let God. I was given jobs for which I did not have to interview, where I met divine connections that served me or that I served. I was so grateful that God would choose to use me in some amazing ways, and there were times I was not so happy to be used, but I learned such valuable things from the seemingly good and bad things. I learned all worked out for my good and that of others when I chose to look for the good in everything. This season of wandering prepared me for service and missions to bless others as well as transforming me. I was so appreciative of an opportunity to rest in peace with God for 26 months of seclusion, even though at first, I was not happy, because it did not appear to be what I prayed for or thought that I needed. I am humbled and in awe of God's grand design and His knowing what each of us need. I am in awe of when and how He orchestrates divine connections and events to get us each to be at the right time, in the right place with the right people for divine advantage and favor.

After numerous divine assignments and 14 months of wandering, I am grateful for each host and employer and all divine connections made during that period. I was so grateful to be blessed with my little one-bedroom apartment, my cocoon with pops of bright yellow throughout, as my place of rest to lay my journey-weary body, soul, and spirit. God is the God of the big and small things and details, this one-bedroom apartment merged together things I had in storage with things I was given. I have learned to be grateful whenever I had much and whenever I had little. God truly provided my daily bread, and I am grateful for the seasons of my growing faith and trust. I am so grateful for great wisdom, knowledge and understanding, which reset my mind, words, thought and actions.

Our words are powerful! They are positive or negative seeds that grow and fuel our thoughts, actions, and experiences. Our positive words nourish us during our metamorphoses and transformations as well as the positive words of others who are connected to us. Whatever we feed and cultivate the most will produce good or bad fruit in our lives and the lives of those connected to us. Connections and disconnections take place in our transitions with people, places, and things in our lives for seasons of metamorphosis. Sometimes these transitions are longer and sometimes shorter.

The quicker we learn to truly let go and let God, the smoother the process of transitioning. Although it causes confusion and still hurts physically, mentally, emotionally, spiritually, and financially. In choosing to be obedient and disconnect from people, places, and things in different seasons we have to remember that He promised us favor. As we open our mouths God will graciously fill them with His word, to help us in the process. The word of God contains powerful seeds to fuel our thoughts, actions, and experiences as we move forward to the new places. He promised he would never leave us nor forsake us and give us peace beyond all understanding in dark places. During disconnection when we are separated and secluded, no one else's words or seeds are able to take root and grow fruit. No one can attach to us a burden, mask, role, or character to weigh down our body and soul. When we try to bear the weight of the outside world and allow others to speak to us, planting words in our minds that grow negativity, we take on their burdens, which we are not equipped to carry. We must ask and invite Jesus in; He steps in as our protector, provider, and Prince of peace, bearing the weight of the world on his shoulders, and disconnects us from the burdens. In seclusion our faith is increased as we look at questions and prayers being answered, building a divine track record to encourage us to press forward when the journey is most difficult, and the prayers are desperate. Also, in seclusion our ungodly soul connections can be cut or broken down, since we are disconnected from others. As we surrender to being secluded and disconnected, we are strategically repositioned and healed of deep-seated mental, emotional, and physical pain.

Sometimes we don't recognize God's strategic positioning in seclusion because it doesn't look the way we think our transformational journey should look. Sometimes it is very ironic, like being a single housewife. It is ironic that I, a homeless real estate broker, found the strength needed in my most broken state to rebuild my new real estate company, out of the midst of the rubble of my shaken and shattered life, from the couch I was renting in someone's apartment. In choosing a new perspective I was able to rebuild my real estate career from that couch, I felt empowered, and knew that I was becoming stronger than I ever imagined I could or would be after enduring and persevering in this process of being stripped bare.

My experiences gave me empathy for others enduring various hardships. The divine revelation I gained from being stripped bare broke me beyond recognition. I felt like a completed puzzle that falls apart into a thousand pieces. The full meaning of being stripped is based on being given a clean foundation to build upon like a divine rebuild. I visualized this season like a rebuild that happens after a tornado has pulled a house off of its foundation. In surrendering to be changed, I gained understanding and revelation that God was putting my pieces back together now and that I would never be the same as before. The full meaning of being stripped like the new house built on the existing foundation has evolved with greater revelation in God's presence. The rebuilding unveiled new anointing, the new gifts and talents to use to be about my Abba father's business in this new season. When I surrendered and submitted my soul and body to my spirit, then accepting and becoming comfortable with my nakedness of being stripped down to nothing, I was elevated, rising to see from a higher vantage point the transitions or journey ahead. Through the destruction of my life and being, I finally accepted my stripping, knowing it was eventually going to be for my good. I settled in for the seasons of seclusion in my little one-bedroom yellow cocoon apartment, disconnected from the people, places and things I knew. As I learned to rest and relax in my seclusion, my very DNA changed and metamorphosis made me a new creature. I have few regrets, since I was covered and protected while transforming and becoming new for my new season. I eagerly awaited my emergence from my cocoon to take flight and transport to new dimensions and illuminate a path for others to follow. In ascension, I acquired the audacity to forge onward and upward on new wings with the faith that I could and would soar beyond my wildest dreams. I reconnected to God in a deeper way with a new approach to my visions, missions, goals, and dreams in my cocoon, where my heart was guarded through disconnection from the outside world.

I know it sounds like just a bunch of clichés, buzzwords, riddles, and lots of metaphors. For those who have walked a mile or two in my pumps, you really get it. I pray grace and mercy over those of you who have not been in my shoes, and that you gain knowledge, wisdom and understanding as a mere observer, to help yourselves or others. My stages of nakedness have taken decades, and it is my prayer that my story will help catapult us forward in our stages of nakedness. I am so grateful my stripping was slow and strategic as it was divinely orchestrated and recorded in black and white on these pages.

Along my journey I was in search of connections and wellness when I experienced my "Biblical Job Moment" in which Keys became very symbolic. Years before this moment I had a big ring of keys for all of my investment properties and a second key ring for my personal keys to my home, my vehicle and my real estate office. Over the years my investment property keys disappeared one by one after divorce, losses, and hardships. Then all of my personal keys quickly disappeared.

The day I found out that my van, affectionately known as Bertha, was not worth repairing; ushered in my "Job Moment." Even though some days I had to lay hands on Bertha, anoint her in oil and pray that she would start and keep moving with only fumes in her gas tank, I was very grateful to have a vehicle without a car payment. Soon after, I had a very troubling day when I realized that, without Bertha's big key on my key ring, I had only a couple of keys remaining. That same week I was fired from one of my temporary jobs, so I had no office key, no van key and the only keys attached to my key ring were a temporary apartment loaner key from my host, my mailbox key that I used as my address, and a storage unit key. I had sent my sons to live with their dad nine months earlier for what I thought would be a few days or at the most a few weeks. As I looked at my key ring, it brought me to my knees. My world was undone, shattered and scattered like puzzle pieces coming apart as it hit the floor. This was my "Job Moment". Yes, I know that Job's situation was much worse, but from my perspective I could relate and connect to Job's story. Never had I envisioned or pictured my world in pieces, and so unrecognizable. After much prayer, praise, and worship, I would pull some of my pieces back together with a new viewpoint and insight, as I slowly moved forward, rebuilding section by section and world by world.

There were many times I felt like I would take a few steps forward only to be pulled two or more steps back like a tug-of-war with pieces pulled apart once again. There were times when my current situation looked like my situation at the very beginning of this stripping process, and it was depressing to think I had made little or no real progress. It took a while, but I realized it was an illusion or veil I had to look through to see why it appeared periodically like the same season or situation. The key was to question, and in doing so, I found the answers as well as the spirits of illusion or delusion hindering my viewpoint. In losing my physical keys I found new interpretations on emotional, mental, physical, spiritual, and financial keys: answers, clues, pathways and connections necessary to freely transition.

My "Job Moment" was a pivotal point in my transition to gain access to my keys for divine restoration. By God's grace and mercy, I looked at each temporary job and each temporary place I stayed in as an assignment to accelerate my development. I asked God what I could do to help improve and what I was supposed to glean from being in these jobs and places with these people. Each assignment brought new keys and tools, and I am truly grateful for the wisdom and understanding gained from each, even though some of the experiences were not always pleasant. These lessons were needed for my growth and development to help me accomplish my visions, missions, goals and dreams, everything for my destiny. Sometimes we earn and learn obedience through the things we suffer!

My hardest lessons were regarding my kids, including regrets from not being able to keep promises that I made to them and the disappointments that they endured due to my struggles. The first few years after divorce it was difficult for me to figure out how to raise three boys in my now single-parent household. I didn't know if I was supposed to be mother and father or what my role encompassed as a single mom or single parent, since they were with me the majority of the time. I was struggling to figure out all of my goals and how to maneuver to keep a roof over our heads and maintain our same or a similar routine at home with them after school, making sure there were as few changes as possible. I had been in counseling to help with the stress of dealing with the emotions of the past and present. I also had my sons in counseling in hopes of making sure they were able to heal and voice their feelings and to be at peace with the new dynamics of our family. When I could no longer afford to pay our counseling fees, we had to stop our individual and family counseling for a while.

We were later blessed to reconnect to a friend who was a pastor, and he became our pastor and counselor, since he was a certified Christian Counselor. He was truly an answered prayer, as God would let him know when we were struggling in any way, shape, or form. He knew when my sons, who were 11, 13 and 17 needed him to speak to them about their behavior, as well as when I was overwhelmed by whatever situation was of great concern, including great fears that plagued me. I spent many hours sitting crying on the couch in his office and then talking with him, finding solutions to the situation at hand. He knew when we needed gas and had no cash, and he would fill up the tank of my van and my son's vehicle. It was a blessing not to have to ask for help, knowing God had heard my prayers and had sent my Pastor to provide gas and food when needed. I am forever grateful that the men and women of God, with our wonderful shepherd, were so attuned with God in prayer that at times exactly what I needed was placed in my hand following church service. I am so grateful for my pastor's and church family's tender hearts.

There were things I wanted my sons to learn as young men that I could not teach them. And these people were great godly role models to my sons as answered prayers for all four of us. It has truly been a blessing seeing how they openly love and serve God. We were blessed to see the walk and talk of the men in our church, to learn from them during our transitions. God was building a track record of answered prayers for us and it was nice to have help and support without always having to ask for exactly what was needed; I did not want to rely on anyone except God. His word told me that He was my provider and that I owed no man anything, but love was truly freeing. There was no advice given that was not from the mouth of God and no strings attached to the provisions given. I had always been a giver, and it was a blessing to see sowing and reaping in this manner.

I prayed for connections with those who had been in my shoes because there was an understanding that comes from walking a similar journey. As I write and look back, I am in awe of the perfect timing of some answered prayers. As each day passed, and I took steps forward and steps backward, I see God's hand in all things, big and small. I realize now that my pastor, counselor, and friend had started preparing me for homelessness by sharing his story and testimony of homelessness. He prepared me for having to send my sons to live with their father and I didn't realize it until later. After our home foreclosed and I lost my job, I sold all valuable furniture and gold jewelry to keep us in our two-bedroom apartment until there was nothing left to sell, and then we were evicted. I tried to find a new place quickly before the eviction hit my credit, but the apartment I thought I would get was given to someone else on the wait list. This process was tougher than I ever thought it would be, and I learned a lot about how foreclosures, evictions and bankruptcy affect you when trying to get a place to live. I found a realtor landlord, who said yes, but I didn't have $7,000 upfront cash. I found another realtor landlord, but after taking my deposit, she changed her mind and chose a 2-parent family to rent her house.

I am grateful for hearing the testimonies of those who endured homelessness and how they made it to their breakthrough. I was so encouraged by the testimonies of others. These gave me hope week after week, especially after I had to send my sons to live with their father. My sons and I spent time together in restaurants, movie theaters, and parks, but it was heart-wrenching not having my sons sleep under the same roof with me. I cried each time I dropped my sons off with their father after our time together. Also, I cried when they drove to see me then departed. I worked hard to keep from opening doors to a spirit of depression and in hopes of saving enough money for a new home for the four of us.

I tried to help other single moms by sharing my resources. I also helped some of my hosts who were having financial difficulties. I learned over the years about spiritual ties and connections that hinder us as we connect to someone financially. We do not realize that we are being hindered in the spirit realm due to some connections. As soon as I disconnected from someone selfish or with a spirit of poverty attached to them for instance, then my finances changed for the better in that season. I learned in the process that it is one thing to give to help someone, but another matter to hinder them or ourselves by creating ungodly soul ties that connect us at a deeper level. We are also affected adversely if someone looks to us as their provider instead of God.

I am so grateful I never had to sleep through the night in my car. I have cried rivers and lakes of tears over the years living apart from my sons. I was not making enough money to change my living situation with the jobs I was able to get, so I returned to real estate. After a year of good rental history, I learned that if my business was not consistently showing income 2 ½ to 3 times the rental amount, I could not qualify as a renter. I so wanted to move back to our hometown where my sons and their schools were located. I had to trust God to work it all out and answer my prayers, as always, to bless the four of us with a home again.

I had to trust God to heal my wounded heart from confusion, secrets, rejections, hurt, pain, usury, sadness, loneliness, disappointment and so much more. I had to remember God's track record with me and the testimonies of others, believing He could and would surely bless me in like manner. I had to spend lots of time in God's presence to find out what His will was and is for me and be specific with speaking and writing my missions, vision, goals, and dreams. I created very detailed vision boards and affirmations which helped to lessen my tears of frustration and feelings of helplessness. I needed a miracle to restore my belongings which had been lost or stolen in what seemed to be constant moves or relocations. I had to submerge myself daily in the word of God to hear Him speak His will for my life and that of my sons. I had to trust God to multiply and stretch the child support or income as I hoped for a comfortable home again for me and my sons in the future. The hard lessons of heart-wrenching pain and suffering through obedience to God ironically brought me lower than I could have ever imagined, and from this rock bottom, I had no place to go but up.

Through the push and pull of repeatedly being moved off course, as well as the roller coaster ride, I was indeed at the bottom, but I was given a clean foundation to build upon as I gained revelation that Jesus is the rock, the foundation upon which we are to build everything and without him we are indeed homeless, regardless of what we own in the physical world. He is the answer to every question, and I was told that I had asked in prayer for many of the situations I had experienced without realizing it, because those answered prayers did not look the way I thought they would appear in the physical world. In darkness and in light, in plenty or famine, and in receiving gratefully all that I needed, I am repositioned and strategically placed to accomplish my purposes, missions, goals, and dreams for my destiny in alignment with God's will and plans for me. I was uniquely and divinely chosen and created ironically to be a homeless real estate broker who has gained access to keys to unlock the secrets to healing physically, mentally, emotionally, spiritually, and financially. We are the sum total of our experiences that prepare us for our journeys. It is necessity that makes us rise to our calling and obedience to the word, and guidance of God which brings mastery in our callings, innate giftings, abilities and well-being.

~Independence Day~

Today, I'm liberating myself to be...Courageous, Beautiful, Whole and Happy. I'm giving myself permission to be...Brilliant, Strong, Trusting and Worthy.

I celebrate my freedom today!

Today, I'm done... Wearing mask, chains and carrying baggage. I am resigning from... fear, shame, and guilt.

I'm liberating myself today from giving and receiving unnecessary apologies.

Today, I will let my light shine.

Today, I'm liberating myself to...Feel, Love, Breathe and Grow. I'm giving myself permission to...Choose, Change, Forgive and Let Go.

I am celebrating my Liberty today!

Today, I'm done...pretending, hiding my magnificence, and being what others expect me to be. I am resigning from... being silent, stuck and obscure.

I'm liberating myself today from giving and receiving excuses.

Today, I will let my light shine brightly.

Today, I'm liberating myself to... be seen, heard and in motion. I'm giving myself permission to...embrace a thought, belief and action.

I am celebrating my Independence today!

Today, I'm just simply done...apologizing for being me.

I am resigning from…being suffocated, being negative and being sorry.

I'm liberating myself today, and because I love you, I'm liberating you too!

Today, I will help you let your light shine too.

Today, I'm liberating myself and you too…you will learn to carry your own damn baggage. My hands are full and there is no room on my shoulder.

I'm giving myself permission to…serve you a notice; that who I was left yesterday, along with your baggage holder.

Contrary to popular belief, I do not have WELCOME written across my back, so kindly remove your feet; no apologies are necessary I know that you are not the one to blame.

Today, this body and these four limbs are my dominion, I am setting the boundaries, and this territory is mine and it is not open for claim.

Today, I'm liberating myself to… Forgive and Be Done!

I'm giving myself permission to…Kick the dust from my feet and let the real me step forward to enjoy this new journey that has just begun.

I am celebrating the brilliance of my light today, because I choose to be Free and to be Indivisibly Me.

Today, I'm DONE…This is My Independence Day!

By Jonquil G.

Chapter Ten

~Bearing It All To Breakthrough~

"I used to believe the purpose in life is to find happiness. I don't believe that anymore. I believe we are all given gifts from our Father, and that our purpose is to offer them to Him. He knows how he wants us to use them."

~Francine Rivers

The Barrier-Breaker will lead them out into freedom. They will all break out, passing through the enemy's gates. Their King will advance before their eyes with Yahweh himself leading the way! Micah 2:13 TPT

We are uniquely made for our divine destinies. God truly does not put more on us than we were made to bear; if we trust Him and let go, He does the heavy lifting or carrying for us. At our weakest point He carries us and our burdens to get us to our blessings. After 14 months of homelessness, I spent about two years being secluded with God. The first week in my own place, I was exhausted from being on the move and on edge constantly. I was glad to have a home of my own where my boys could come and go freely, but sadly I did not get approved for a safe, clean place for the four of us to be comfortable near their schools. I slept, then prayed and slept and prayed more the first week. I was in pain and my digestive tract was a mess due to all the stress and changes in life and to my diet. I felt bad for the first few weeks in my new place, but after a few weeks everything was released - toxins, stress and all the spiritual hitchhikers that were stored in my body, and I started to feel better. I decided it was better to limit time spent with anyone with negativity or drama in their lives so that I could recover and heal. I found that as I focused on different lessons, I learned while wandering. I gained insight for my mission. Keys were revealed or given to me to assist in healing all areas of my life.

I took 10 bright yellow poster boards and created very detailed vision boards for each area of my life to make sure I was in alignment with God's desire and blueprint for me. I prayed, then I built these boards weekly, awaiting guidance. Even the name of the new apartments I moved into was a key for me, showing me what God was doing for me; the name meant Ascension. I was sent to a place to rise to a higher level and restore part of my life. After having my vision boards on my bedroom wall for almost a year, I evaluated what I had accomplished, and which goals required tweaking after more prayer and guidance from the Holy Spirit. I knew and continuously spoke over myself that this was my season to transition, transform and be restored. I even had a vision board for my celebrations after my achievements were accomplished. I realized it was better to say season than month or year, not knowing God's timing regarding these visions. Also, I allowed very few people to see my boards, since people sometimes act supportive, but then, out of ignorance about the power their words carry, might speak negatively over our visions or missions, effectively cursing them. I believe we must seek to rejoice in something each day. Once the day is gone, it is gone. Journaling, putting thoughts and dreams on paper, can be a pathway for our wiser self to uncover. A letter becomes a word which becomes a concept, a sentence, a chapter, and a book by using everything as our daily bread for each day.

If you consider that our bodies are majority water, and if you think about the fact that God spoke over the water of the Earth to create, then we must be careful what we allow to be spoken to or over our water. I previously spoke of being with unequally yoked people and I started evaluating relationships once I was in my place of peace, focused on my vision and missions. Being restored meant I could position myself for the home God promised through his word as well as the words from the mouths of His prophets, and provide the peaceful harmonious lifestyle that God desires for my sons and me. It was imperative that I spent time with God to focus on my God-given blueprint intently.

It was imperative my sons have tenderhearted godly role models to mentor them and I realized it was imperative for me, as well. I started realizing my seclusion was needed to see clearly both naturally and spiritually what was being entertained and allowed in our lives. We get used to pain, for example, and after a while we don't notice we are hurting. We don't look for the source of the pain, and we accept it as commonplace in our lives. Emotional and mental pain shows up in our bodies, but until we remove ourselves from everything and everyone, we suspect may be the trigger, we can't see or hear clearly to find the cause of the pain. We all have brokenness; none of us are perfect and should learn not to judge. But like attracts like, and when we are overwhelmed and in pain we don't evaluate well, especially when we get stuck in a mode of pleasing people. Priorities must be set, and most important is to decide to put God first and spend time with our maker to know who he created us to be and what he created us to do. We are social beings, and we sometimes stop building a relationship with God, our Creator, in exchange for many relationships with others that are not as fulfilling. We lack fulfillment in relationships because we are not in alignment by being connected first and foremost to God who then connects us to others.

At times along the journey, we look back at the past, at times we focus on the present, and at times we contemplate our future, but it is very important we do not dwell in the past, which is done and gone. The paths are laid before us where keys are found to unlock doors to mysteries and hidden treasures. Trades are made along the way, some good and some bad. Masks and façades are revealed. Untold stories emerge as letters become a word, a word becomes a concept, that concept becomes a sentence, and those sentences become a chapter then a book by squeezing out of each day all of its essences in the present moment before they become revisited past or contemplated future. Essence exudes from broken façades to lay bare before the eyes of God and others the buried treasures and mysteries. We learn to excavate layer by layer to uncover connections and roots. We learned to endure suffering like pulling off a bandage, whether slowly or quickly, to expose a wound to air and light for healing.

Along the journey we become aware of hitchhikers, ungodly yokes and soul connections that encumber our movement. Becoming bare leads to the ability to break away, which releases us to breakthrough. It is imperative we do the work needed to open our eyes as we become naked and unashamed once we are bare. As we are released from our self-imposed prisons that veil our insight and cloud our judgment, we start to think clearly and desire freedom. Deliverance and healing go hand-in-hand like deep wound cleansing and care for inside-out restoration. We must see clearly to become aware of who, what, when, where, why, and how to break away. It happens stage by stage, season by season and revelation by revelation. When we suffer a long time, we may forget our mission and become stagnant in mediocrity.

In our suffering, we sometimes lose sight of our vision. Our passion is limited when we are unsure of our purpose. If we lack prosperity, we are delayed in what we believe are our dreams, and we sometimes spiral downward quickly as we are delayed in our mission. Over years of suffering, hardship, disappointment or whatever we choose to call it at that point in life; breakthrough is very elusive. By the time we think we have arrived at a breakthrough, we realize it has eluded us once again. There were days when I was sure of my purpose; I walked and talked with passion and felt productive and prosperous. Those days I walked and talked positively, I did a good job loving others and myself. There were also days where I spoke that God's plan sucked and I felt horrible; on those days it was difficult to be obedient, loving and to have faith in his plan. While in seclusion I would think back on those days and events that I didn't understand, finding it was hard to encourage myself. Some of those experiences were actually for my benefit. Suffering makes us try most anything to break away and break through hardship. At times I was thankful to have made it to the next minute, hour, day, month, and year; at times not so much. Some days were glorious, breathtaking, and beautiful! Love fuels our purposes and missions; faith keeps us moving and working God's plan, and hope assures us of our destiny. Over the past decade I was in search of "The End" for this book, my story, and my breakthrough. I was looking for my happily ever after! I believe breakthroughs lead to new beginnings in each moment, day, week, month, and year, which then hold new breakthroughs. Our purposes and His plan for our destiny is filled with faith, hope and love, all those are needed for breakthroughs.

Over the many years of writing, I found myself wondering where all of the hard and soft copies of my book were located, knowing that not all had been updated. I wondered how I would feel if they were lost or if I were not able to finish after decades was poured out on pages and it was not able to help those it was meant to help. I have prayed, repented, read books, and sought-after instructions from seers, prophets, and pastors in search of confirmations, connections, steps and anything to help with the elusive breakthroughs for manifestations of victory. I was in search of ways to please God in order to achieve breakthroughs in every area of life. I was in search of how to be in this world but not of this world, as well as how to relieve the pain I felt when disconnected and out of balance physically, mentally, emotionally, spiritually, and financially. I was in search of how to seek the kingdom of God and what that truly meant in regards to life here on Earth. I found that it all boils down to having relationships that positively move us along his plan. Relationships are a struggle at times, because we are human beings and not perfect. Even our relationship with God feels difficult at times due to the struggle with alignment of our body, soul, and spirit. Like any other relationship, the one with God is constantly evolving as well. Learning to trust God is the key to unlocking peace in spite of how bad or glorious it feels at that time on our journey. Transparency is needed to develop sound relationships that are reciprocal in nature. Relationships make our lives worth living and bring adventure to your journey. It is imperative to stay connected to God and in daily communion with God. Notice who you spend more time with: God the father, Jesus or Holy Spirit and get to the root of why.

Our connection or lack thereof with Abba father, the Holy Spirit or Jesus reveals things to us if we engage, each person of God. When we realize that we have a lack of intimate deep connection with God, we gain revelation of our relationship issues with others. Until we rectify the relationships issues we have with God, the other relationships in our lives suffer. When we are struggling in our relationships with God, we sometimes substitute other relationships, and we may hold on to those we should release. Many times, we have misdirected expectations, and when people we have saddled people with unrealistic expectations and they don't fulfill them, we think we are not liked or not loved. Some days I felt like I had been kicked in the stomach or I felt like an elephant was sitting on my chest. The pressure and pain were sometimes unbearable when I allowed the stress of some relationships to hijack my peace. God knows what we each need in our relationships and our transitions: either to forgive and connect or forgive and disconnect. I am so grateful for the decades of development and the stages that I went through. There were seasons of connections then seasons of disconnections. I learned discernment during all of those seasons, and I gained understanding. I transformed and gained knowledge about healthy and unhealthy relationships. I also learned about godly and ungodly connections and ties.

As the eyes of our understanding are opened, we see all things in new ways. The more intimate our relationship with the Lord, the more Revelation we gain as we process information coming to us in the natural and in the spiritual. God is the master restorer, and in His hands, nothing is wasted. He will repurpose, restore, regenerate, restructure, and rebirth so that old things become new, stage by stage. He can restore everything lost, stolen, devoured or damaged. When we surrender in the Master's hands to be restored, the obscure and hidden gifts, talents and anointings are revealed. As we arise in confidence in our newness, wisdom and amazing works spring forth. Our faith is built as we step forward and embrace our restoration. We are able to step into our preordained destinies as revelation and words of knowledge direct or guide us to flow in gifts, talents and anointing that were not utilized prior to rebirth. It takes time to learn and get used to the new you; newly repurposed, restored, regenerated, restructured and reborn. It feels like getting to know a new friend. The wisdom of our preordained destiny is within each of us, and when we are functioning at the most authentic level of who we are destined to be, there is a sense of déjà vu. We all in our gut have an innate knowing of when we are doing what we were created to do and be. The spirit of intelligence and the spirit of the wisdom of God is activated through being in God's presence and putting a demand on ourselves to rise to a higher level. That's when supernatural increase happens, as well as the manifestation of miracles. It should not be extraordinary, but ordinary to see and walk daily in the supernatural as mature children of God. We must speak to hear, as faith comes from hearing. We must also see with our divine imagination that which we have heard ourselves speak to walk as wholly restored and new beings, learning and functioning in our anointing or God-given abilities that do not lift off of us. The wisdom of God helps us to rise above the issues of the world and to walk in our anointing to help fix our issues and the issues of the world and continuously change the world for the glory of God. I found that breakdowns bring breakthroughs.

Breakthroughs are large and small but we must recognize the small ones. They appear as open doors for our readiness to receive the new transitions and new opportunities of favor. This is the year of the Lord's favor; I've spoken this for years but have been seeing it more lately. I started this book with Proverbs 23:7 "For as he thinketh in his heart, so is he" (KJV) as well as some questions that started my awakening. In chapter 1, I stated that wellness is a choice. Choosing a positive mindset and desire to assume responsibility for or give permission to ourselves to transform and heal as we transition through life. Through observing and interviewing women over the years I am able to see connections, roots and fruits to assist God as he calls me to help in the deliverance and healing of others. Questions have led me to answers, roots and fruits. I have found the secrets to deliverance and healing in those questions and answers, roots and fruits or disguises, hindrances, delays, and attacks. I see deliverance as revealing our secrets, removing masks, chains and baggage, which opens gateways for healing.

I see energy and connections to people, places, and things like a matrix of spiderwebs; intrinsically designed pathways and points of connection as a master plan or blueprint for each of our lives being weaved as we go through life expressing our free will and trying to align with God's will for our destiny. I believe God wants to use us to serve one another by assisting when and where it is necessary for the deliverance of others. I have spent years removing masks, chains and dropping baggage to become untethered from hindrances. It has been a long process for me and others to get free and walk in healing and prosperity.

Many are in search of a pathway or connection to a prosperous, purposeful, and passionate life. Over the years my thoughts changed regarding the depth of what it means to have a prosperous life. After being homeless I learned to be content and grateful for every little bit of grace and mercy I received. God was keeping me safe, providing and teaching me over the months in the different places I slept and in the many different places where I worked during those months. I was so grateful to have a place to call mine again where I could sit for hours in prayer at rest and in peace with God. I learned to live by the Spirit; to walk in the fruit of the spirit… Love, joy, peace, patience, kindness, goodness, faithfulness, gentleness, and self-control. I have a picture that has the fruit of the spirit on it that I have spent years staring at. I've asked God to help me do better in living by the spirit and expressing this fruit in my life. Be careful what we speak and pray for, because it will manifest, and the process may be lengthy. Seeking to walk in the fruit of the spirit became my pathway, and I realize I have a prosperous life. My values changed and I gained things that money cannot buy, such as the spiritual fruit plus wisdom, knowledge and understanding at a much deeper level. I know money is necessary, and the more we have the easier it is to serve and help others with financial issues, but it does not deliver us or heal our body and soul. Wisdom, knowledge, and understanding are needed to be good stewards of wealth in order to assist in the kingdom of God. The worldly view of a prosperous life encompasses financial freedom, but if we are not walking in the fruit of the spirit, we are probably not walking in our purpose and our life probably does not have passion and purpose.

Some people have financial freedom but are not living by the spirit and are not spending enough time developing a close intimate relationship with Abba father, Jesus and Holy Spirit. It is very difficult to live our destiny, the purposeful life we were uniquely created to live, without God. Passion comes with our intimate relationships with God when we are in alignment with Him as our creator. It is like a pen trying to write on its own without the author and finisher. I believe God is the author and I am the pen, ignited with passion for God and through God as I work purposefully serving others with the knowledge that God has blessed me with a truly prosperous life of peace.

In this chapter of life, revelations are springing forth from my heart as I gain new insight into connections, life-giving relationships, and inner gifts. I see Isaiah 61 speaking of a purposeful, prosperous, and passionate life. I have spent years studying this chapter of Isaiah; it spoke to my spirit and of my life. It spoke of my service, my ministry, my purpose of being sent to help the brokenhearted. I want to proclaim freedom for the captives who do not know they are captives, like I once was. My passion and purpose are to help provide for those who grieve, and to remind others of our inheritance and promises. Our Lord is just and faithful and will bless according to his everlasting covenant with us and our children. My Lord Jesus will make righteousness and praise spring up as I spring up in full bloom for all to see. I had to be delivered from spirits of fear, torment, shame, and guilt plus a slew of others due to soul connections, generational curses, alliances, allegiances, dedications, and contracts. I had been working on this culmination of stories for a long time, but I was anxious at times about finishing it, especially because I had not achieved certain goals, and certain visions had not yet manifested. I was looking at this as my story and I did not know how to bring it to an end, because there was a new chapter always starting. So, my perception had to transform in order to release these stories, connecting and healing myself and others as a blessing to the world.

Bare is about uncovering and sharing women's journeys through struggles such as abuse, obesity, illness, depression, fear, financial issues, career changes, divorce, widowhood, disappointment, and dissatisfaction. My goal was to joyously and triumphantly embrace and walk in transparency or nakedness - as these pages illuminated my pathway, and that of others. Some are stuck, stagnant, or hindered, and others are flowing freely and smoothly from stage to stage as they transition. Those willing to do the hard work, choose to uncover secrets and pull off the layers of masks and crud in order to find their new self. We are blessed greatly as we bring forth and deliver to the world the treasures from within our earthen vessels. Delivering a purposeful, prosperous, and passionate life that is revealed, restored and reconciled for healing in all areas of life.

A pivotal point for my breakthrough of final layers of restoration or restructuring happened as I learned about the Courts of Heaven. I could see where delays took place due to legal rights and accusations in my life and the lives of others. In all of our lives I saw patterns of prayers being seemingly unanswered, delays in destinies, and cycles and issues continuing. I read several of Robert Henderson's books on The Courts of Heaven and I started researching to get through stages and remove more layers. I was desperate for solutions to end cycles of despair, disappointment, and dissatisfaction in many aspects of my life. I knew that to help others get free I had to be free, since only free people can free other people. I was desperate to get my prayers answered and see manifested blessings in my life to propel me forward in my purposes. I was also desperate for a deeper understanding of the kingdom of God, which came as I researched The Courts of Heaven and how to function in the heavenly realms. I had questions that were answered through visions and visitations with God. My spiritual senses were honed as I studied to gain depth of understanding of the kingdom of God. I learned to connect the dots as I prayed and listened for the root causes of legal issues causing delays on Earth. I gained a deeper understanding of the Lord's Prayer in Matthew 6, especially regarding "on Earth as it is in Heaven", to gain divine advantage for declaring and decreeing from the second realm of Heaven in the Court of Accusations. I was desperate to walk my walk and talk my talk as written in black and white and to be set free and to help others become liberated as new creations, joyfully walking in each of our preordained divine destinies.

~Oh! Her Struggles!~

As awakening begins her eyes are opened to see her struggles are more than just a few.

Oh! Her Struggles as she sits and wonders; how will I make it through the heartaches and pains from years of hidden abuse?

Remember my sisters, God brought you to it and He'll bring you through it.

Ask? Just ask, His promises are yes and Amen.

Oh! Her struggles as she sits and wonders; how will I make it through the heartaches and pains from food and alcohol misuse?

Remember my sisters, God brought you to it and He'll bring you through it.

Ask? Just ask, His promises are yes and Amen.

As awakening sets in, her eyes have been opened to see her struggles are more than just a few.

Oh! Her struggles as she sits and wonders; how will I make it through the heartaches and pains from having few marketable skills and feeling as if I am of no use?

Remember my sisters, God brought you to it and He'll bring you through it.

Ask? Just ask, His promises are yes and Amen.

Oh! Her struggles as she sits and wonders; how will I make it through the heartaches and pains of having bill collectors calling, my credit score falling and compromises to be made for bills to be paid as I feel my spirit begin to reduce.

Remember my sisters, God brought you to it and he'll bring you through it.

As awakened now until the end, her eyes are opened to see her struggles are more than just a few.

But now I have seen all that God has brought me through and I know that through his glory and grace my blessings flow profuse.

Ask? Just ask, His promises are yes and Amen.

By Jonquil G.

Chapter Eleven

~Ordinary To Extraordinary~

*"Go ahead! Take the leap of faith! Your feet will never slip!
God will stabilize your every step! You will quantum leap
into higher and greater realms of authority, influence,
success, and prosperity! Stay focused! Be encouraged! Don't
give up on your dreams!"*

~Juanita Bynum

[18] "Do not remember the former things, or ponder the things of the past. [19] "Listen carefully, I am about to do a new thing, now it will spring forth; Will you not be aware of it? I will even put a road in the wilderness, Rivers in the desert. Isaiah 43:18-19 AMP

It is my hope and prayer that this book has blessed you. It was a labor of love for almost two decades as it was my journey of discovery and transformation as I learned to be unashamed of my testimony. I did not realize that it would take so many years for me to transform and give birth to this book, my written record, my black and white road map of the race that showed me where I had come from, and where I had arrived. It showed me the intersections along the road that were pivotal points, tipping points, points of divine advantage and connections. It helped me to remember experiences that startled me into awakening, those experiences brought great enlightenment of divine connections and God's favor. I noticed the connections freed me and healed me, as well as some others along my pathway. I found great revelation and keys to help me connect and be present in the current moment. I learned to follow the Holy Spirit in order to avoid getting stuck in the past when examining those things that had taken place before. Through guidance I learned how to stay in the present moment to gain instructions, so that I do not forgo the opportunity in that moment to change the trajectory of my future. I learned the perfection of now, the perfection of the current moment, and the mercy and grace to choose how I look at and live in any current moment. Some days I lived moment by moment, then when strengthened I was able to live day by day, choosing to speak into existence the goals and visions I believe God planned especially for me. Each day is an extraordinary new day of connections to see everything more clearly through brave new eyes that are wide open with awareness of the divine, renewing our perspectives of a grand design that empowers us to live more brilliantly.

My ordinary days became extraordinary when I was led to a prayer room near downtown Dallas after viewing a video of the worship team. The Lord told me to go to that prayer room. I was living at the first location of my second season of homelessness at this time. Upon arriving, as I prayed, I asked the Lord what was delaying my progress or forward movement. Then a few minutes into worship I had a vision of a large spider on its very large thick web blocking my path. The Holy Spirit told me to pray in tongues and as my prayer intensified, the spider and its web rolled up then disappeared. Days later, I had another vision that was even more clear. I was drawn like a magnet or a moth to a flame to another prayer room, north of Dallas. I was instructed by God to spend my days in the prayer rooms writing, studying and praying intercessory prayers. At the beginning of the third month in the prayer rooms, I asked the Lord what I should do regarding income and He told me, "I am your daily bread, your protector and your provider, and I will direct your steps." I decided I would be more obedient than ever before; no matter how things would look to me or others who shared their thoughts, opinions, and advice with me. I decided I would trust the Lord and I would be more obedient than ever before, no matter how I felt. I was only instructed once to ask a Pastor whose name God spoke for gas money. The lovingkindness he showed me as he looked at me with great compassion tore down walls, I did not realize were surrounding my heart. When I had need of food, gas, or a simple desire, the Lord provided. Without my asking, people would hand me what I needed saying, "The Lord told me to give this to you." In the past I had been blessed here and there, but this was different, and the needs were provided sometimes immediately after I thought or quietly spoke it to the Lord.

It was truly extraordinary to see the hand of God move on my behalf, showing me that He would do what His word said He would do. I was told by God to compile a list of visions, dreams and prophetic words given to me so that I could speak and declare His promises in that season. It has been amazing to see manifestations. I am so very grateful for this season of rest abiding in His presence with other intercessors. I am so grateful for each time I questioned if I should remain in the prayer room or seek temporary employment in an effort to restore the real estate company the Lord gave to me. While in one of the prayer rooms God sent different prophets to tell me to be still and continue to rest in His presence and trust Him.

During the fourth month, the Lord sent a prophetic message after I asked if I should change my occupation to be a full-time intercessor, since I had been in the prayer room for several months. I heard the testimonies of several who were paid intercessors like in the day of King David. I desperately wanted to please God in every area of my life and I was will to change everything. I went to the altar to be prayed for as I received the prophetic message that stated, "whoever is in real estate as an agent or investor, God is going to touch your work in this industry and you are going to experience increase in this season. I had just asked God days before to tell me clearly if I should pay the upcoming renewal fee to keep my real estate license. I wanted to surrender my license and submit to the Lord in order to be completely obedient to whatever the Lord was calling me to do at that time. My clear message came like a neon sign the day before my license renewal date. The Lord provided the funds for my continuing education real estate classes and for my license renewal fee without my asking anyone. He touched someone's heart to provide, showing me, he was in control of it all. I call Jesus the CEO of this real estate company that He gave me to steward or manage. Over the years God shifted and changed how I function in business. In this season he chose to restructure how I am to work real estate His way.

A week after his neon sign prophetic word in the prayer room, I was asked to set up a meeting with an investor I had prayed for at a birthday party a month or two before I got this clear confirming message. During the set-up time for the party, I shared part of my testimony of homelessness with them. Then at the end of the party during clean up I asked if I could pray for the hosts and investment partners before leaving. As I prayed, glory dust from Heaven that looked like micro jewels of various tones was sprinkled on the small group, showing the presence of the Lord blessing all who were present. The Lord put me on the heart of one of the gentlemen, reminding him of my story. He told me that he set up our meeting because the Lord told him to help me. So, he offered me a position with a salary, stating he wanted me to pray and intercede for his business endeavors. He stated that he knew I was called to work for the Lord first and foremost and we could figure out the details of my salaried position around what the Lord called me to do. During the meeting I told him that I was a licensed real estate broker, and I could help with his real estate investments. I was in awe of what the Lord was orchestrating and how it was being structured around my being in His presence in the prayer room.

To spend my days as an intercessor would have been an answered prayer after the past few months of continuously being in the prayer rooms seven days a week all day. I realized how much I enjoyed it and was gifted to remain in the presence of God for long periods of time. My long-awaited prayer was to be blessed with a new home for my sons and me. During the meeting, this gentleman told me that God put it on his heart to help me get a home. I had heard stories of people who were blessed in this way, so I praised God.

The following week I signed up for my continuing education real estate classes, and all went well day one. But day two started out with a battle just a little over one hour before the start of my state regulated class. I walked out of the house where I was staying temporarily to find my car gone. I called the police and found out that my car had been repossessed. Since I was at a temporary location, I thought it would not be found by the loan company while I awaited my first paycheck from the investor, but they activated the tracking device and towed it away in the middle of the night. By God's favor and mercy, I was able to make it to my class, but I met with spiritual opposition throughout the whole day. A couple of hours before the class ended, I had a food allergy reaction and struggled to breathe while dealing with stomach pains. Text messages regarding my address and car only added to my distress. I realize that I had been asking God to remove stress, debt, hindrances - all old things, and bring all new things with freedom and peace. I realized I should not have been surprised that the car was gone, even though it did not take place as I thought or prayed. I surrendered the car saying "Lord, you work it out", if I am to reclaim it, then provide the finances". But God reminded me that I had asked for debt to be removed. The car was the last of those debts, so I learned to be more specific in my prayers. It was very humbling asking for a ride to various places, especially after having my own vehicle since I was a teenager. It was very difficult, but I learned to adapt. I certainly got healthier as I walked for both exercise and to go shopping for my needs. I had chosen not to tell or discuss in great detail most of the trials, tests, and events that occurred over the past two years, prior to finishing the conclusion of this book, unless prompted by Holy Spirit to share parts of my testimony to help someone who needed to hear it.

Because I did not fully understand where the Lord was taking me, some days, weeks or months it was very difficult to talk to people and answer their questions regarding work, a vehicle and housing. Most of the time I knew the answer to questions regarding work. I knew that I was an employee of the Lord. But because most cannot see my boss, they thought I was unemployed. Some could not see the work that I was doing or the value in that work that I was doing, especially knowing that I was not getting paid for many of the tasks that I was doing. I was seen as and called lazy, sometimes politely and sometimes not. God provided for me through small real estate transaction fees so that I was able to stretch my resources and provide nice meals for myself and hosts. As I shared my testimony or things that I learned over the years through my experiences, I was practicing to be a voice in the body of Christ. As I shared my expertise, gained while I was being equipped to consult and coach, I was also equipping others to function in the body of Christ and to function doing business in the Kingdom of God. I have found that some people who do not have similar experiences to mine are curious and have questions such as "Why I am going against the grain or doing things contrary to the actions of many in society?" My goals, dreams and visions are similar to those of many people, but my action plan has changed from me deciding what and how to accomplish the goals to asking Holy Spirit to lead and guide me in His action plan. God gave me a blueprint that fewer than 5 people were given an opportunity to glance at over the years. As I learned to ask daily questions in preparation to build my business and ministry blueprint, I was given instructions and my tasks for the day. This book is a major part of that blueprint. I knew that as I wrote text messages or emails of encouragement or correction for people, even chapters for this book, as I meditated on the Word of God, as I learned new things like healing modalities, studied life coaching information, learned more about cryptocurrency, researched property information, and prayed with and for others, I was working for the Lord Jesus my CEO. I learned not to worry about finances, but rather trust that He would provide and remember that He has provided necessities in various ways. Trials teach us who He is in our lives and helps us gain understanding and empathy. Trials also teach us to be quick to listen and slow to speak, so that we may hear Holy Spirit first, in order to properly discern the spirits behind our own situations or those of others.

I mentioned in the previous paragraph about no longer having a vehicle. As I write this paragraph, I am in awe that I have been able to remain at peace without a vehicle for almost 2 years. The only question that I have been asked mostly with a puzzled look regarding a vehicle is "Do you not have a car?" Not having a car has taught me patience while I wait for those who are kind enough to occasionally take me places. I found ways to do what I need to and get what I need within walking distance, and by God's grace He has placed me in homes near shopping centers. I desperately missed having my own car, especially when attending spiritual events with others who want to leave before it ended. I do not like to leave a spirit-filled event until every bit of glory has been poured out in the room and I have been able to part take of each tasty drop for refreshing my battle-worn soul. I have also learned patience as I await God's promises that He would provide me with a debt-free vehicle and home. So, I will trust God as I await His directions on when, where and how to receive my blessed vehicle. The investor I mentioned earlier from the party was not obedient to God and did not keep his word about the job to intercede and assist with real estate investments.

Even though I had experienced homelessness, I didn't truly understand the levels of homelessness until I did research. The US government's definition of homelessness is when a person lacks a fixed regular and adequate nighttime residence, and if they sleep in a shelter designated for temporary living accommodations or places not designated for human habitation. There are 3 types of homelessness: chronic, transitional and episodic. The categories or levels of homelessness are 1. Homeless according to the definition, 2. Doubled up: These individuals split costs by sharing a dwelling, the person with better credit and adequate income being on the lease, and the other having a lack of security and opinion or responsibility in the dwelling, 3. Couch surfing: Relying on the kindness of others for temporary stays determined by your hosts, 4. At risk: Due to living one to two paychecks away from being homeless, occurring in the case of a major traumatic event or natural disaster and 5. Hidden homeless: When two or three families share a house or apartment without the other families named on the lease. Any disagreements could launch the other families into a different level of homelessness. Some of the causes of homelessness are death, divorce, illnesses, substance abuse, felonies, excessive hoarding, damages done to properties, rental issues such as evictions and foreclosures of both houses and apartment complexes. My search for better understanding revealed that the US states with the highest numbers of homeless people are California, New York, Florida, Texas, Washington, Massachusetts, Oregon, Pennsylvania, Illinois and Colorado. Negative effects during and after homelessness, such as fear and paranoia, and low self-esteem, causes some to breakdown and become institutionalized, or result in a loss of will to take care of oneself, hoarding due to a fear of loss of possessions, increased possibility of danger and abuse, possibility of kidnapping or murder, increased chance of entering the criminal justice system, behavior and social issues due to traumatic events, loss of faith, and hopelessness that sometimes leads to suicide.

The first 14 months I could not stand to hear the word homeless. Every day I was just trying to keep my head up and not drown in defeat and depression as I experienced several levels of homelessness, such as hidden homelessness, where I rented a room in someone's home. I also experienced being doubled up and couch surfing or a variation of that, when a bedroom was provided temporarily for my use. By the grace and mercy of God I did not experience being on the street in the elements day and night. For one six-week period, due to parking issues at my host's apartment complex, I had to park my car at a 24-hour shopping center and then get a ride back to the apartment. I also had to stay gone during the day since she was gone during the day and she became paranoid that her apartment managers would find out that I was staying there without being on her lease, so I would pack whatever I thought I might need for the day and I left when she left. I also found that if my host had not been self-employed, or they did not see what God was doing with me, they assumed that I was not working if I did not leave the house or apartment as they did daily. As soon as some expressed those thoughts, I knew they assumed my being on my computer writing or doing marketing was play, not work, and shortly after, God would move me. During this very difficult 6-week stay due to the mood swings of my host, I had to go to libraries, parks or visit friends if I did not have appointments, since I had just started my real estate business again. Plus, I started investing in cryptocurrency with a friend during those weeks. I was exhausted after that 6-week stay from being on the go constantly. During those weeks I realized that homeless people needed to be creative and resourceful to find places to work, eat, and use the bathroom, as well as sleep and shower. I was very grateful to realize how blessed I was to have a car again and a place to sleep and shower as I learned all that God would have me to learn during those months. I saw homeless people that seemed to be continuously on their feet and on the move due to business owners or police telling them to move along from various spots. I also saw during those months how substance abuse causes family, social, physical, mental, emotional, spiritual and financial issues. My discernment increased with each move as I gained knowledge of the issues that plague women who have experienced levels of homelessness and the negative events and effects that linger for years after homelessness has come to an end. I found that the vagabond spirit attaches to the homeless, and it opens the door for more spirits to come in, getting deeply entrenched and setting up strongholds. Having personally dealt with this vagabond spirit, I have gotten well acquainted with it, its strongholds with other connected spirits, and soul connections that occur in people with similar situations, as well as how to deal with it in deliverance sessions. I find that some of these women have deeply rooted fears of being homeless again and anger towards God that keep these strongholds in place, causing illness and dis-ease in their body and soul.

I was so grateful that God led my host to recommend I apply for a second-chance apartment complex. I was a real estate broker, but I did not realize the difficulties faced by people with rental issues such as foreclosures, bankruptcy, evictions or felonies. I had leased my rental homes to people with bankruptcy and foreclosures as well as evictions if they had stable rental history over the past year and seemed to have a good reason for the hardship. I found through personal experience that a foreclosure counts as an eviction, since the banks file for eviction to get a person or family out of a house. I found out that most apartment complexes in my area require at least two years of good rental history, and that you have consistent income of at least 3 times the rental amount. I learned numerous things that as a landlord I never contemplated or considered, but these things were used to deny me lodging as a tenant. I was approved to rent the one-bedroom apartment by the favor of God and given a chance, if I was able to pay a security deposit three times the amount of the deposit those with good credit history would pay for the same apartment. It is very difficult to get good rental history if no one will give you a chance to rent, especially if one cannot meet all of the criteria. I was desperate, and I could not endure another day in my current situation. So, to meet the criteria of 3 times the income I asked an acquaintance who owned her own company to write a letter for me stating that I worked for her company, and the pay was 3 times the amount of rent. God provided exactly what I needed financially during the 3 days that it took for the complex to get the apartment ready for me. Near the end of the 26 months that I was there, I experienced being at risk of homelessness again, due to my shrinking savings from being self-employed and no new house sales. I learned so much about the process of eviction. Because I asked the Lord for help when I saw that I was in danger of being evicted, I was led by God to a non-profit that helps tenants fight eviction by knowing the laws and certain papers to file. I was able to remain in my apartment, because I sold a house that enabled me to pay back rent owed, and by God's grace the late fees were removed by the general manager. Then months later I had clients that went to other agents or chose not to purchase at that time, and my savings was depleted. I prayed and fasted, asking God to provide supernaturally and help me to stay in my apartment. The complex assistant manager who handles evictions did not give me proper notification of eviction, which I knew well from having been a landlord and from the information gleaned from the non-profit. When we went to court, she lied and had false documentation, stating she had followed the process so it was my word against hers in court and the judge ruled in favor of the complex. This happens much of the time when tenants do not know their rights and the correct procedures to follow. I left the court room, evicted with just enough to rent a truck and a few days to pack my belongings and move. While sitting in my car I asked God "Why did you not help me in court?", and I clearly heard, "A lie got you into the apartment, and a lie took you out of the apartment." I asked for forgiveness for the lie and repented. Having learned a lot about the eviction process from both sides, I also learned a very valuable lesson regarding the enemy using evidence in the courts of Heaven which manifests on Earth as it is in Heaven. Once repented, the evidence is not of use to the enemy in the courts of Heaven, and I believe Holy Spirit and angels are able to intercede on our behalf here on Earth. I realized that I prayed and asked God to provide favor for me to get approved for a second chance and I asked for the finances for the deposit but I did not ask for help with the criteria of income being 3 times the rental amount, so I followed the advice of man, not God. I lied and took that matter into my own hands, turning in the false documentation instead of trusting God with everything in that situation, so a lie and false documentation took me out of that apartment.

I learned that the number one reason women become homeless is due to domestic violence, as many have to run for their lives, and sometimes to save their children or spare them from hurt and harm. Through talking to many women over the years, I found that for many, a combination of reasons leads them into homelessness and may keep them homeless for weeks, months or years. In previous chapters I spoke of women who were homemakers, housewives, domestic engineers or soccer moms who agreed to give up their careers to take care of their children, home, and make life easier for their husbands as they focused on climbing the corporate ladder or building companies. These women later found themselves obsolete in the job market. Many are lacking experience to gain a job in their previous field. Depending on when or how young they were when they got married, some women did not work long enough to gain enough knowledge and expertise in a field to have a resume that would gain them a job that would keep them in the same lifestyle as they had while married. Many become unemployed or underemployed, even though they may have great skills gained by managing their homes or helping their ex-husbands with their jobs or businesses. Some must choose new careers that have them travelling to make a decent income to support themselves and their children. Some women take jobs that keep them on the road most of the time, so they give up a place of their own, utilizing the saved income to provide more for the children, pay child support, or help other family members who care for the children. There are At Risk women who invite homeless friends or acquaintances under their roof in hopes that they can work together to split the expenses, arranging their work schedules to cut childcare costs by caring for each other's children while they each work the necessary hours in hopes of being stable, then thriving someday. Sometimes these women who are givers end up with women who are takers, and all hopes are dashed as the givers end up in a worse position than when they moved in together, especially when the takers are plagued with spirits of poverty and selfishness. When At-risk women bring takers into their homes, they most likely all end up homeless due to the unwillingness of those that they invited in to create reciprocal relationships. Some At Risk women who take in homeless women and their children and are later devasted to find out their children are being stolen from, bullied, abused or raped in their own homes by the other children they graciously invited in. Others find themselves working so many part-time jobs to keep a roof over their family's heads that they need day and night childcare help from family and friends. They are heart-broken when the reality sets in that they barely see their children and worse, when they look up from years of the rat race to see that their children are now grown and they have missed so many milestones and events trying to provide necessities and a few desires for their children.

Moms in circumstances after divorce or the death of a husband without adequate estate planning, inadequate life insurance, lack of retirement funds and worse, an unknown mountain of debt, find themselves in a deep financial hole, drowning in debt without the income to escape that bondage quickly. There have been some women and their children who have had to move from their home after divorce or death. They have to sell their house if they are not able to afford the payments, and/or maintenance costs due to a lack of funds coming into their now single-parent household. They are sometimes in shock if everything happens quickly and they have to change their lifestyle. Is it shocking to anyone just to move from a large home to a small one, but unfortunately, many people have to move from a large home to a small apartment. Apartment living is very difficult to get used to if you have always been in a home with the freedom to make noise or enjoy quiet, but in an apartment, you have to learn to tolerate the noise of others, especially apartments with little insulation or soundproofing. Tragically, some families move to a hotel before they end up homeless shortly after the divorce is finalized or the funeral is over. It is scary and shocking for those women and children going from a home to an apartment to deal with the common constant rotation of neighbors. It is far worse for those living in hotels, because their neighbors change daily or at most weekly, coming and going next door to them. These women do not know from one new neighbor to the next if their family will get adequate sleep due to the loudness or vulgar language or noises their children will be exposed to daily coming from next door. Some women find that during or after physical or mental illnesses they end up homeless. Some experience additional traumatic events that take a toll on their limited finances or uninsured or underinsured assets. Accidents, fires, or natural disasters can be the final nail in the coffin. In some cities there is a lack of affordable houses to rent, affordable apartments and affordable hotels which causes more homelessness in those cities. Some women move to a new city or to a new state for a new start and a new job, but if that job does not work out as they had hoped, they find themselves and their children homeless without connections, friends or family near to help.

I pray that these paragraphs have been eye opening regarding my experiences and that of other women I know who also experienced homelessness for various reasons and causes, as well as dealt with negative effects and challenges associated with being homeless. It is my prayer those who have not experienced it will learn to be more sensitive and to pray before making comments, judging, or asking questions that insult the intelligence and question the sanity of the person enduring levels of homelessness. I was asked if "I chose to be homeless instead of getting a permanent residence?" My answer is No, knowing what I know and have experienced I believe no one in their right or sound mind would choose homelessness instead of getting a permanent residence with rights, security and freedom to have privacy, invite friends over to talk or for dinner, freedom to decorate the space to your taste, freedom to have out of town guests stay and freedom to nap whenever you want or need to plus so much more. I was most saddened by the fact that most of the places where I stayed, I did not have the freedom to spend time with my children in homes of my hosts. I do not know any women personally who have chosen or prefer to remain homeless, doubled up, couch surfing, At Risk or the hidden homeless. There are some individuals and families living in hotels and motels, which I did not understand the first 14 months, since I only stayed in the extended stay hotel for one week. Because they have few choices, a hotel or a motel becomes their residence as they wait a couple of years to be given a second chance if they had rental, legal and financial difficulties. One issue with living in a hotel or a motel is that it sometimes causes more issues because in most cities the cost is so much more than an apartment. Here in Texas, after someone has lived in a hotel or a motel for 31 days straight, they no longer have to pay the taxes; they pay only the base room rate for the number of people in the room.

I have also found that Holy Spirit will touch the hearts of some to give money to help someone in a crisis or during transition, but later when the spirit has lifted off of them, they start questioning why they gave and will ask questions that make them feel bad, upset or regret for having given to someone who is in a situation that they have not experienced and do not understand. Some offer to give but put stipulations in place for the recipient that causes more stress to already stressful changes in the woman's life. I believe that I had not really lived, learned or been truly liberated until I lost everything and had to start over with a clean slate, trusting God for my daily needs and desires as everything in me and my life was made new.

As I reflect back on my past experiences, I realized it was imperative for me to be willing and fully surrendered as well as obedient to follow God's leading with child-like faith. Only God knows every detail of the plans or road map he has for me. God is the only one who can rightly lead me step by step not my family, friends, acquaintances or even myself, so I decided to let the Lord shepherd me without the influence of others' thoughts, opinions, questions or advise, regarding certain situations. I awaited confirmation from prophets who did not know me or my situation to serve as my guideposts of alignment with the plans of God for me. I found that in traversing new pathways it is best to keep my business between me and God, telling my testimony only when prompted by God to those travelling companions on my path. When prompted I share my testimonies to encourage those who God has passing by me on the barely used narrow pathways in sometimes-dark seasons. During long transitional periods with little change in my life it was very difficult talking to people who focused on the ordinary and were clueless to the extraordinary and not grateful for the little things. People are so busy running the rat race that they take for granted the miracles in nature and daily life, at times I was focused on the wrong things also. It takes great sacrifice and determination to walk in faith, pressing forward against the grain of worldly views and appearing foolish while speaking and believing the same things year in and year out with few visible changes and droplets of blessings.

I believed that the floodgates would open soon and that the droplets of blessings were from the movement of the floodgates of Heaven, and I encouraged myself in solitude. I believed God would bless me with a car and houses again that were paid in full in the right season, which was shown to me previously in open visions. I knew it had happened to others, so I believe it could and would happen to me too. Some days I could see the looks of pity from those who had heard my confessions of belief in the miraculous, stating year after year that God would restore all that I had lost as many saw my situation get worse and not better. Sometimes shame came in, knowing that many thought I was delusional as I spoke things that were not as though they were visible to all. Others times I stayed secluded to avoid naysayers and to enjoy the peace of speaking and encouraging myself in the Lord, knowing that His word is true. As I await manifestations, I know that in the right season all that I have experienced and written will help others, and as I speak my testimony others will be uplift as their faith is increased, knowing that God will provide for them also, according to His promises.

I started walking in the wilderness years ago, when I became homeless and had to send my sons to live with their father. It was a step-by-step process of learning to trust God not only for my daily bread, but for everything. During this season of intense prayer, praise and worship, God orchestrated divine connections. In the meeting with the investor, I was offered a salary plus commissions, as well as office space for my real estate company. I was also offered a house and a car as we discussed my car repossession. After our meeting, I asked God what type of car would I need in the new season then I went and chose my new car, signing in faith all of the paperwork. God had also led me to a house that I liked months earlier that fit the description given by a prophet 3 years prior as it was being built as a model home when the prophet stated that God was building a house for me. Over the months I asked the Lord to bless me with that home for my sons and I. I realized that this could possibly be the house that the prophet spoke of, as it was built the year of the prophecy. This was one of many houses that I looked at and prayed in over the years since my house was foreclosed upon, asking the Lord to bless me with a new home for my family. Over the years after losing our home, I tried to figure out how God could do this for me, and I tried to help Him by telling Him what I thought would work best for the orchestration of the payment of the house and car. I was able to believe that God could prompt this man to be a blessing to buy a house and car. After all, he contacted me and told me that God put it on his heart to offer; I did not ask him to do it. A few times now I believed that God was providing my new home and a car through men and or programs, so I previewed houses that I liked. It was very disappointing when the purchase or program did not manifest. I have taken my youngest son with me on several occasions to preview houses, asking him to have faith with me for our new home, so it was most disappointing knowing that he was disappointed too. God's word says to ask, believing in your heart, and it shall be given to you. So, I asked God to make it so and I set my heart and mind to believe, paying no attention to naysayers who thought I was being gullible. I have found that men change their minds for various reasons and programs come to an end, especially when Holy Spirit is not constantly involved, consulted and Jesus is not the CEO. But I knew my God was unchanging and His plan or program for me would happen. I had nothing to lose and everything to gain by casting all my cares and concerns on my miracle-working God. It has taken quite some time for me to simply trust in God and His word, not concerning myself with how His divine orchestration would manifest all that He promised me.

Two weeks after my car repossession, the investor meeting and my visit to the car dealership to choose the car I desired in faith, I was taken to the emergency room by my sons and hospitalized for pancreatitis. My ER doctor, told me that my lab results and behavior did not align with what he had been taught and experienced over the years, and he wanted to know what made me different. I asked him to explain his concerns to me so that I would understand his question. He told me that he had seen people with Lipase numbers far less than mine who were not coherent or pleasant. My lipase enzyme total was at least 5 times that of most people he had seen and commented on my being pleasant in spite of my pain level being at 10. He asked what was the difference in me and I told him I have spent months in prayer in God's presence constantly in prayer rooms. He told me that he had heard and believed prayer makes a difference but he had not seen evidence of it like in my situation. I was put in a hospital room to be observed constantly, and I told my sons not to worry, but to go home and rest for their work and classes.

After my sons left, I started talking to God, asking Him why I was in the hospital and would I be okay. I asked Him to help me understand why after months in his presence; what was I supposed to do in this hospital from bed? I dozed off, then someone came in to draw my blood. I asked how his day was going and he said good but I sensed it was not going well and told him that, then I asked if I could pray for him. I knew then what I was doing in the hospital. I was on assignment, but I was not sure the details or extent of my assignment. I awoke when the door to my room was opened by a doctor who said his name was Dr. Wright or Dr. Right, who told me several times that as the doctors come to my room no matter what they say to be at peace and remain calm. I thanked him and he repeated "be at peace and remain calm no matter what they say" then he left my room. My nurse came in saying they were about to change shifts and she would bring in my new nurse to introduce us and that the doctors would start doing their rounds soon. I told her that Dr. Right had been in to see me already. She said excuse me and walked out. She came back moments later saying that there was no record of a doctor coming in to see me and that they did not have a Dr. Right. I told her that I believed God blessed me by sending an Angel to ease my mind and heart by telling me no matter what the doctors say I am to be at peace and remain calm, I told her after giving me this message, he walked out of my room and headed to the right, away from the nurse's station. I sent text messages to family and friends asking for prayer, especially from the intercessors I had been praying with over the past few months at the prayer room as I awaited the doctors. The Lord touched the hearts of several intercessors to come in to lay hands on me and pray. Several even came in and sang over me, and as they laid hands on me, I felt my organs vibrate. I noticed over the five days in the hospital, I was prayed for, then I prayed for the hospital staff that came into my room.

The day before I was hospitalized, I had gone to hear a Pastor speak on meditating on the word of God. After he finished speaking, I told the Pastor that I did not feel well and I was struggling to drive to his meeting because I had stomach pain. He prayed for me and told me God was calling me to a fast and I should ask God what type of fast, as well as when to start. I had days before had a dream where Jesus was in a doctor's white coat. I found it ironic that I saw Jesus in a doctor's coat, then I was told to start fasting because once hospitalized I was put on a dry fast of nothing by mouth. Days later I had microscopic surgery to remove 2 gall stones from my pancreatic duct. As God spoke to me and intercessors came in to pray for me, confirmations came from God that I would not need another surgery. God put it on a friend's heart to tell me that He told her to take care of me once I was released from the hospital. I knew the Lord had used her in the past to bring healing and reduce swelling in my lower right leg that had remained swollen for years no matter what I tried due to the numerous car accidents. I knew it was best for me to accept her offer of care, since she understood what God was doing with me to prepare me for women's ministry and kingdom businesses. On the day I was to be discharged, she did not return my text messages or calls, so I started wondering what would be the best plan B. I did not want my sons to worry about me, but I was at a very low place, since so much disappointment had hit me during that month. My sons came to pick me up once discharged from the hospital, and they dropped me off to have a different friend wash and deep condition my tangled hair. She took care of my hair, and while there I got the confirmation call that everything was arranged, and she dropped me off to my place of respite and recovery that I called my upper room, since it was the only room on the second floor of my friend's rental property.

Over the years, as I learned to listen to God to do and go where Hi called, I found that he always blessed me with confirmation, especially of major decisions. In this upper room I was able to rest and recover on my own terms with the peaceful presence of the Lord. Over the weeks of recovery, some days I was amazed as I watched new assignments unfold as the Lord revealed things during my solitude and seclusion. It was a blessing to have food dropped off as my friend would check to see if I needed anything, then leave me to peacefully rest. I started sharing my experiences of visions and time with God in the prayer rooms with my friend's daughter, who then asked that we all go to the prayer rooms and bible studies together, which fed her spiritual hunger.

I noticed that I felt a lot of movement in my gut, similar to the feeling of a baby kicking, but I knew something was not right. My friend's daughter was having difficulty with her relationship with her boyfriend, so I told her I knew of a counselor who could help them. I knew she needed deliverance, but realized as I spoke to the Minister, I needed more deliverance also. So, I set up an appointment the day before my young friend so that I knew what was in store for her. It was a huge blessing to each of us. We were catapulted forward towards our callings with new revelations. I felt that

I had been derailed by decisions I made that did not align with God's instructions for me, and I felt that the same was true for my friend and her daughter, as we all had various sessions of deliverance. I was able to be present for several deliverance sessions which was very helpful as training. It took weeks for me to realize that this house was located in the same area as a bank where I had my first job after I was divorced. I believe I was brought back to the area where I was derailed financially years earlier to make peace with my past. I gained so much revelation for my preparation and equipping while in the upper-room of that house.

As I look back at my life, comparing 2008, the year I got derailed to the years that followed, in the eyes of many my life might seem far worse in the later years. In 2008, I started working a job that I detested, that I only applied for out of fear, but that was used for my good. I was on an emotional roller coaster because I had a home and I had my 4 rentals, but my tenants were moving due to chaos that was unfolding in my life and business. I had a job with a salary and child support and I started writing this book from my journal entries. Months later I was trying to figure out how to build a new real estate company, after being fired from that job, which was a blessing because I would not quit even though I was spiraling downward suffering from illness due to stress. Once again, in fear, I went into the insurance industry, since I could get a draw on my commissions. I had acquired investment licenses while at the bank, and was quickly recruited by an insurance company. It was a great learning experience both personally and professionally. But I realized I did not like it when policies were cancelled and I was working, but my commissions weren't enough to offset cancellations, so I was finding it difficult to pay my bills.

I decided I would have faith and figure out how to get back to real estate sales, which I enjoyed. Plus, there were no charge backs of commissions in real estate. There was no residual income, either, but charge backs were difficult to deal with since many of my clients were struggling single moms and I felt bad for them - and me - when they had to cancel policies. Over the years, I was involved in numerous multilevel marketing companies and in and out of real estate. Through an acquaintance with one of those companies, I met a friend who was also in real estate, and God used her to get me back in real estate as we went to the altar together after hearing the prophetic word at the prayer room months earlier. Several times over the years, I had asked God to give me a neon sign if I was really supposed to remain in real estate. Previously, I mentioned that a few years ago, I asked God for a neon sign with real estate. I see that over the past few years I was trying to make sure that I was doing what and going where God wanted me to, according to His will not mine. It was a difficult process of learning to trust and be a peace with God's will and not be upset or disappointed with how things manifested. A prophet and friend were my neon signs to remain in real estate over the years. It took me a long time to realize that as a single income household with my income being 100% commission and experiencing feast or famine as the market changed, I needed to create other streams of income to survive. Once my business entered a long season of famine with delayed closings, then no referrals or sales leads, I became homeless again. Unfortunately, I kept rebuilding my real estate business or creating witty ideas and inventions, but I kept going through the same financial struggles even though I had a tenacious grip on the promises of God there were issues with implementation of the strategies I used in business and inconsistency in my habits and schedule due to struggles emotionally and physically. I am so grateful and blessed that I have not had to sleep outside. The Lord has provided safety and a reasonable amount of comfort.

I started walking out my crazy faith in a different way during this second bout of homelessness, trusting God would answer my prayers. I did not realize moving out of my apartment and in with a friend was an answered prayer to help me with this book and the women's ministry originally started in 2009. I moved into my friend's home a week before Christmas, doing everything I knew to do to trust God in the process. I realized later I was there for a spiritual education to help with my book and prepare me for ministry someday. The Holy Spirit called her the librarian since she had collected many books, DVDs and digital information on various subjects. I was with her for almost 9 months when my pancreatic attack and hospitalization shifted me into Dallas where I had worked a decade earlier. I moved into a friend's investment property in the room dubbed the upper-room. My friend had other friends temporarily living in the lower level of the house. It was a blessing to be there with them during my recovery, because there was someone to help me. I was so blessed to have peace and quiet to hear God in the upper-room.

Weeks after being discharged from the hospital, I met a nurse at a prayer room. I told him about my pancreatic attack, and he said I was a walking miracle because the patients he had seen with Lipase numbers like mine had been in a coma, then died. The breakdown of every area of my life has been an amazing process of preparation through deliverance and healing. I learned who I am with and without material things. I also learned to be faithful to God as I was stripped Bare, uncovering my brokenness. I spent the last weeks, while recovering in this upper-room, mentoring my friend's daughter and other young women as they visited. I had received several prophetic words about mentoring spiritual daughters. The Lord used this upper-room as these women came to visit and spend the night showing me what my women's ministry would look like as I helped women deal with emotional, mental, physical, spiritual, and financial crises. I am so grateful for all the little blessings and signs that the Lord heard my prayers. Over the past decade, as I awakened into the knowledge OR awareness of who the Lord created me to be and what to do; I found peace beyond understanding. Helping these young women helped me better deal with the time away from my 3 sons as I mothered them. I would hear God telling me that he would take care of the 3 children that He had given to me as I helped those that He sent to me.

While in the upper-room, Jesus kept beckoning me as He said come up here and let me show you how it looks from a higher perspective. I awakened to see that the beauty in my wilderness experiences had taught me very valuable lessons I could share with those who crossed my path ready to receive these pearls of wisdom I had acquired. I learned to trust God no matter how the situation appeared from my current perspective because He sees and knows the beginning to the end. In my new beginning I am now equipped and prepared to walk out the plans the Lord had for me in this new season. My equipping and preparing came at a high cost, and I chose to follow Jesus obediently no matter how it felt or looked. Even when the investor did not do as he had said that he would, I knew that man's words, thoughts and promises are subject to change but God's are the same yesterday, today and tomorrow. I was shown many years ago by God the vision: a blue-print for my destiny, but my memory only recorded a small portion of that plan I prayed for clarity then I put that vision on paper like a pictorial business plan of the women's ministry and businesses to support it. As I was obedient in my daily walk with Jesus, I did not even think of the vision or the plan given to me years ago. I was willing to give up my vision, previous roles and jobs to follow Jesus, doing his will and not mine.

The prophetic word about real estate did move me back into real estate once again, but this time I kept the Lord first, remaining obedient to His instructions on how, when and who to do business with, whether clients or industry partners. Then a specific prophetic word came to me to look closer at my vision and blue-print because this was the season for it to be birthed. Over the past decades I tried to bring forth different parts of the vision, but the businesses or ministry would not flourish. I found the pictorial vision in my computer and as I looked closer at it, I saw things with new eyes unfold before me, and it included far more opportunities for blessing the kingdom of God than I had seen in the past. I became acutely aware of why I had to learn to trust God for my daily bread and learn daily obedience in all things as I looked closely at the extraordinary God vision that was unfolding before me.

This manner of equipping and preparing was a must for me in order to walk on this pathway to birth with the Lord every part of His vision and plans for me. I was being taught to be in the throat of the body of Christ as a voice in this season. God chose me to speak with fire as the sword of the Spirit comes from my mouth. I will teach and coach others from this book and workbooks, as well as whatever God places in my heart learned through my suffering and triumphs. During the months of recovery from my pancreatic procedure, I attended a conference about walking in intimacy with God, for the purpose of deliverance. My companions and I were then sent on a deliverance mission by God to undo, nullify, and revoke bloodline curses, and dedications. We headed to Kansas City, MO and Kansas City, KS for 3 days. I had been in Kansas City 15 months earlier on a mission to share what I had been learning regarding the Courts of Heaven and spiritual warfare, so I figured that was the open door, or beginning of my mission, since part of that trip included deliverance and healing work. I was surprised that the hotel my companion booked was in the same town or suburb that I had previously stayed in during the last trip to Kansas City. As we prepared for the trip God, started giving us the same or similar instructions, even though we were not with each other while we packed. I asked God to provide financially for our trip and He did through a love offering from a friend after I helped her with some deliverance issues, so I accepted it as a blessing and answered prayer from God to help pay for our hotel stay.

Our room wasn't ready when we arrived at the hotel, so we went to a nearby park to walk after the long drive. As we walked through the park, we saw the playground, and since no kids were on the swings, we recalled childhood memories as we hopped on the swings and soared in the air, giggling with delight. I believe the reconnection with childhood ignited our child-like faith during the swinging and kicking through the piles of crunchy autumn leaves. We fasted and prayed for the first day and a half of our trip, doing everything God instructed us to do without question: just a giggle here and there of the oddity of some of the instructions. In our obedience, I was reminded of Isaiah 55:8 "For My thoughts are not your thoughts, nor are your ways My ways", declares the Lord. I believe that when we are faithful in the small things then God can and will trust us to do the big things in our missions. I also believe that when we risk everything to follow God's instructions the reward blesses us greatly emotionally, mentally, physically, spiritually and sometimes financially.

In the process of this mission or training, we were able to go enjoy a wonderful museum event. It was so inspiring, prompting me to think about trying new art mediums. Art therapy had become a big part of my healing and restoration process, especially while in the upper room as God used my young friend who is a very gifted artist to teach me a few basic techniques. God moved supernaturally in both Kansas City trips, and this one with the movement of the Holy Spirit, Angelic presence, and healings. Various things I had seen in my dreams and visions that were playing out in the natural world reminded me that everything is a part of our training in some way, shape or form. After we had completed our mission in Kansas City, MO and headed onto the highway, my companions and I saw a homeless man with a sign on his bike asking for food. We had food in the car, and traffic was at a standstill, so I got out to give him some food. After I handed the food to him it felt like a hand hit the middle of my back, shoving me to the ground as I began to run towards the car that was now four car lengths forward. I looked over and up from the ground at the man, who was asking if I was okay. After I stopped sliding across the pavement due to the force of the shove, I struggled a few seconds to get to my feet, because I could not put any pressure on my left hand, which I knew was broken. I got up and ran to the car, and once inside announced to my companions my hand was broken. My friend is a licensed massage therapist and had been a physical therapist so she started pushing bones back in place as God guided her hands. When she was done, her daughter began to pray and remove the trauma from my tissue, joints and bones as she moved and manipulated each finger and tendon of my hand, then wrist. Guided by the Holy Spirit, they worked on my hand. I spoke to my hand and commanded it to be healed and totally restored in Jesus' name. I spoke to God asking what I was supposed to learn from this experience, and he told me it was so that we could all practice and learn more about healing and miracles. My broken hand healed in a few days, and only a small bump remains as a reminder of my miraculous healing.

My miraculous healings helped me be obedient and willing to trust God's instructions especially since I was led back to real estate even without a car. It was a perplexing part of my training to walk in faith. Nothing is wasted, and the ripple effect of many of the things that we do out of obedience are not even realized. We are rarely aware of all of the points of connection to the people, places and things that are used to strip us then restore us to true wellness. Sometimes it takes years before we see full circle moments of connectivity and gain revelation from an accumulation of knowledge assimilated to solve issues. Once we truly understand connectivity and wellness, we are able to remain at peace, resting in the arms of Jesus even in the midst of storms that turn all our worlds upside down mentally, emotionally, physically, spiritually and financially. In the eye of the storms with Jesus is where we gain depth of wisdom, knowledge and understanding of the matrix of connections, intrinsically designed pathways and points of connections as a master plan for each of our lives. Our master plans are being woven as we go through life obediently, joyfully and faithfully following the directions given to us by God, expressing our free will or His will for our destiny. As we rest with, in and through Jesus, we humbly accept our missions no matter the cost. Even when storm winds are fiercely blowing, we see from his perspective that these winds bring much needed or prayed-for changes. We forget that his angels come as winds or fire and although these winds and fire may bring destruction, they also bring the new things needed or create the ash for new growth to begin.

I found that in getting to the eye of the storms the winds were used to strip me of old things, move me to different places, and blow in new people as connections needed for the next stage of development, preparing and equipping me along this master plan of my destiny. I am so thankful for all of the prophets placed along my pathway that gave prophetic words which served as bread crumbs to lead me to the next point of connection to the right people, places and things for that season. Over the years, I was broken in different ways and cried many tears as I opened doors to fear, shame and guilt, enduring periods where I missed family and friends as I was without transportation. But through it all I was able to gain the characteristics, perseverance, wisdom, skills, and humility to be used on missions by God, learning to give Him all the glory in my testimony. I can see my pathways and pitfalls throughout these pages, showing when I was stuck in loneliness and bitterness. I could see all the roots and connections to unforgiveness, resentment, rebellion and anger that I repressed deep inside that erupted here and there like a volcano spewing idle and profane words. I also see when I developed in the Fruit of the Spirit; love, joy, peace, patience, kindness, goodness, gentleness, faithfulness and self-control. As I look over my journey in black and white, I am in awe of God and all that He has done to, through, and for me to bring me contentment in my close walk of fellowship and friendship with Him.

I am expectant in the dawning of each extraordinary new day. I am so grateful for every part of my journey of awakening into the continued awareness that I am the sum total of every experience. I am thankful for all the connections which brought wellness and understanding that truly being who God created me to be means being…Bare, Brave and Brilliant for His divine use in the Kingdom of God. I do not remember not knowing and not being connected to Jesus, but this past decade has been truly amazing, especially all that I learned during 2020. He walked and talked with me as these chapters unfolded. I have always loved books, and over the years The Lord directed me to books that greatly helped me make connections for deliverance and healing. I will list at the end of this book a few that I believe would be helpful for you. I find that God gives us what we need when we need it is for our destiny. Throughout the past year of this season there has been an acceleration and intensity in the lessons I learned.

The Lord has given me everything needed to gain revelation for my destiny over the years. As poems were revealed that served as therapy for me, they were compiled to become a Poetry Journal. That became the first self-published part of this Bare Series, and this book is the second. There will be other books and workbooks to follow as additions to this series. These evolved from exercises, experiences and encounters over the years that helped me find extraordinary supernatural connections. It is my prayer that this series will be used as transformational guides for a smooth transition to your destiny! It is my hope and prayer that you will Dare to be…Bare, Brave and Brilliant too!

Over the past decade I was greatly blessed by God, who provided my daily needs, especially over the past few years, like literal daily manna from Heaven. But I struggled with truly receiving in my heart that I was worthy of a second chance with abundant prosperity. God had sent numerous prophets who did not know me or my circumstances to tell me messages like I am special to God, I am the apple of his eye and it is His will for me to prosper. I found that sometimes I figure out my issue watching or listening to someone else. We can speak with our mouths all day every day but until we start with our hearts to address the issues of our hearts and the mind-heart connection we will not find healing in our financial world. We must deal with bitterness and unforgiveness of ourselves and others for mistakes made, unkept promises and ungodly beliefs surrounding finances. Like layers of an onion, we can believe we have been healed emotionally and mentally but when dealing with money some find that soul ties are rooted deep from many years of living in vicious cycles. These issues or soul connections are from childhood. Many times, we don't realize that connections from our past can affect our present and future finances. We need to properly deal with these soul connections as soon as we notice them.

In this new day know that you can have whatever you say! It is sad that those who are not walking with Christ have utilized spiritual laws to prosper and the children of God are deceived into accepting into their lives lack and poverty as if they are badges of honor. I decided I would stand on this verse for newness in all areas of my life.

Isaiah 1:19 TPT [19] If you have a willing heart to let me help you, and if you will obey me, you will feast on the blessings of an abundant harvest.

A fragmented heart has trouble hearing and receiving the word of God in order to bring forth fruit for a thirty, sixty or hundred-fold harvest. Also, a fragmented heart that does not truly understand generosity, they may be obedient but not willing, generous and not cheerful, or question why they should give at all. These different soul fragments only understand in part. For example, they may see God as a healer of disease and broken bones but not as the one who can and will raise the dead, or as the supplier of new body parts. The seeds of faith are the same as we grow, and we can develop them the same by repenting, by letting go and letting God, by binding and loosing, by giving, by joyfully walking in faith, and positively speaking. We must declare and decree with authority the word of God and His promises over our lives and all connect to us.

The Lord knows my name and the doors to open for me. He also knows your name and the doors to open for each of you. He is shepherding and leading me as I travel the pathways designed to equip and prepare me for my destiny through doors to help lead and guide others on how to surrender and submit to being stripped. I previously mentioned reflecting upon relationships with Abba Father, Jesus, and Holy Spirit to gain understanding of set-backs and hindrances in life. As we develop and grow intimate connections and relationships with our triune God, we must evaluate or examine our worlds in connection with those relationships. As Jesus reveals Abba Father to us, we get a better understanding of Mark 11:27 as well as the other verses in the New Testament where Jesus and Paul refer to God as Abba Father.

I see Abba Father as the Father of Fathers. As I come through Jesus the door Abba Father joins me to himself spirit, soul and body as I give myself wholly to Him, confidently seeking a deep intimate relationship of trust. I learn to understand the spirit of adoption and receive the Spirit of God into every part of my soul as Abba Father is revealed by Jesus to me. I truly became a son of God and mature in sonship as I learned to ask, seek and knock, understanding Abba Father more deeply by connecting and spending time with Him. I must receive with all my heart that I am a son of God just like Jesus, with birthrights, knowing all things are possible as I am wholly connected to Abba Father. Our preordained birthrights are in the word of God. We just have to speak them then believe them with all our hearts. Romans 8:15 is a very freeing and empowering verse because it tells us an adopted child has all the same birthrights as a natural born child, and according to Hebrew roots, it appears they have even more rights. As we truly receive this verse in our hearts, its truth can surely deliver us from limiting beliefs and mindsets. We can believe the promises of Abba Father as we follow His spirit, seeing the ordinary as extraordinary, and becoming more like Jesus each day. God is our everything: friend, husband, savior, redeemer and so much more.

Chapter Twelve

~Manna And Miracles~

"When we lose one blessing, another is often most unexpectedly given in its place."

~C.S. Lewis

"You provided bread from heaven for them for their hunger, you brought forth water from a rock for them for their thirst, and you told them to enter in order to possess the land which you swore to give them. Nehemiah 9:15

As I stated previously, the Storm of the Century in Texas brought me from a conference in Houston to a motel near Dallas. I spent 81 days learning to be still and know God as my provider of daily manna. I learned that he is the same yesterday, today and tomorrow. Just as he provided daily manna in the wilderness for the Israelites, he also provided daily manna for me during my wilderness seasons. Also, just like He provided quail when the Israelites cried out for meat, he did the same for me as I cried out for various things. I am in awe of the favor not only of God, but from man, that I experienced at the motel. The storm ushered me into a new season of discovery with God; learning more about Him and myself on my daily walks with Him. The storm also ushered in new extraordinary things and experiences, taking me and my prayer partners to extraordinary new levels in the spirit realm. I found it ironic and amazing that the condo was #107 and the motel room was also #107. For 81 days room #107 became my prayer room, my sanctuary, my refuge and my respite to gain strength, skills and more revelation from God to continue my journey through to manifested restoration. Revelation sprung forth often with my prayer partners, and as I utilized these new or deeper truths, I gained confidence and courage to continue my journey step by step and day by day. As I put aside the old words, thoughts, deeds and desires of the past and embraced newness, I uncovered things I did not realize were connected, increasing my knowledge base and faith. During those days my skills, talents and discernment were sharpened in the areas of gifting for my purpose, and calling, preparing, and equipping me for my God given missions. I hoped and prayed that my restoration would transition me from the motel to my new home, the one that had been prophesied by several prophets over the past six years. But, to my surprise! I was directed to a homeless shelter as the place that would usher me into my restoration in all areas of my life. Everything is a part of our training in some way, shape, or form, and we must be willing and obedient to follow the leading of God, even though it may be perplexing.

As I was divinely guided and moved from the motel, I was directed to a homeless shelter that I did not want to go to because I remembered donating to it in the past, and it seemed very dark, depressing and full of dark activity. I was told that it was really nice now and the buildings were new, so I decided to get some information and to check it out. In little confirmations God showed me this was indeed the right place and the right time to connect to the right people and right things that I needed at this point on my journey. It would provide what was needed for the final stripping of all pride, shame and embarrassment. It would also provide the training I needed for increased discernment. I started seeing many wolves in sheep's clothing and goats thinking they are sheep. Many of these people desperately needed deliverance and healing but they have no clue that deliverance is needed. Many speak like Christians, but unfortunately cannot pretend 24/7, and the façade crumbles down, leaving their brokenness on display for all to see and hear. The poison from their hearts rises, and comes out of their mouths, revealing their true colors. It is apparent in the words and actions of those who do not truly know Jesus and his ways. They are not guided by, nor do they exhibit, the fruit of the Holy Spirit. This was a time for me to learn to walk in extraordinary compassion and empathy for those here who are angry and filled with pride, shame and embarrassment too. Some here lost grip on life balance and well-being, living totally deceived by the enemy. Many remain stuck and sinking below the strongholds and delusions due to laziness, unforgiveness and so much more. These wolves in disguises have turned manipulation and usury into an art form, taking advantage of those lacking enough discernment to see the puppets of the enemy delaying, deceiving, and destroying the destinies of those on big missions for God. I found myself really struggling by my third week of living in the Inn because facades had come down for many, so I found myself judging and lacking compassion. I found myself behaving very indifferent towards others here. I also struggled to fast and pray in this place at this time with these people. At this crucial time and place it was prophesied I would receive restoration beyond my wildest dreams as I cross over and through this Inn. I was hoping to be able to pray and fast, bringing my supplications and pleadings before the Lord, in order to press through this most difficult phase of my journey. I was so hoping to go from the motel to my new home, but found myself dwelling in a facility with hundreds of strangers. These strangers are from all walks of life, ages, ethnicity and cognition. It is my most difficult task thus far to not only dwell here but to find empathy and compassion for some people that I simply find hard to like or tolerate. My previous roommate during the pandemic was used to prepare me for this season with these Inn-dwellers, since she was previously an Inn-dweller too. I am grateful that God used her to prepare me and assist in my finding the ability to show lovingkindness to someone whose actions and habits I found intolerable or disgusting at times because I struggled with OCD cleaning issues at times.

I found it very humbling and difficult to deal with my time being structured by the program and directed by staff, changing the house rules at will, relishing in lording over those who were down and out. I found that I was getting agitated due to all of the spirits and personalities in that Inn. I also saw that Inn was a refuge for those coming out of the Nut house and the Jail House with ever changing rules and favor. The constant fluctuations of people, both staff and residents, kept the Inn-dwellers on edge. The coming and going of roommates and rule changes was difficult because by the time you got used to one stranger or strangers in your room, you start all over again with a new person or persons, and being written up for not following the ever-changing rules. In that shelter I have seen the best of people and the worst of people. I have shown my best behavior and worst behavior as I was constantly poked by puppets of the enemy. It was imperative to remember that these people some coming from the nut house or the big house are all divine connections to assist in deliverance and healing from pride, shame and embarrassment, and to bring lessons for discernment and strategies which lead to restoration and connections for wholeness.

"He knows about everyone, everywhere. Everything about us is bare and open to the all-seeing eyes of our living God; nothing can be hidden from Him to whom we must explain all that we have done." Hebrews 4:13 TLB

We will all come before God Bare; stripped of facades and the things of the world. We all have some areas of our lives or places we want to avoid. I desperately wanted to avoid going to a homeless shelter. That was rock bottom in my eyes. Just like the Israelites avoided going through Samaria, even though the road from Judea to Galilee went directly through it, so too did my road to restoration go directly through that shelter. I never dreamed that I would need these Inn times in order to be prepared and equipped for my mission, ministry, manna, miracles and even my future marriage to the man that God gave me the name of in February 2010. Those Inn times stripped me of pride, shame and embarrassment as well as rejection, and cut the connections with many ungodly entanglements. I felt under so much pressure in that place due to changing house rules, so many dark spirited people practicing dark arts and enduring community living with so many broken Inn Dwellers. In that Inn seeds were broken to produce better and bigger Fruits of the Spirit, like lovingkindness.

That which the enemy means for harm God will indeed use for our good by causing the importunity needed to increase the forward movement of continual prayer. Importunity brings continuous asking until we receive. Also, importunity brings continuous seeking until we find, and continuous knocking until all of the doors with our names on them open wide. When the doors with our names on them open they reveal and manifest all that was promised to us through the word of God and through His prophets sent to us. Importunity ushers in urgent persistent solicitation or demands as one presses forward into God to the point of being trouble-some or annoying with shameless insistence for favor, like the unjust judge who finally caved in to the widow's demands in Luke 18:1-8.

I stayed focused and pressed forward in fervent prayer by being an importunate person. It was very difficult at times until, like a moth to a flame, God led me back into the prayer room. I believe increase and manifestation came as a result of focused fervent prayer, and ushering in the presence of God to bring Heaven and the things of God down to Earth. Importunity became a key to manifestation of my restoration as prophesied by the word of God and by the many prophets sent my way over the years. Importunity brought about fullness of time or God's perfect time with the right people, places and things. The discomfort of community living and the sharing of living space with strangers seemed harmful at the time, but ended up being a blessing. I learned more about compassion and showing lovingkindness to those strangers from the nut house and from the jail house with whom I dwelled. Many of us had different walks of life, socio-economic levels, and other variables, but God saw fit to lead us all to that right place, at that right time with those right people that brought me into importunity.

The culmination of these frustrations caused the urgency, persistency, and fervency of prayers, affirmations and declarations into the atmosphere of that shelter or Inn of Increase. As I reflect and look closely at my journey of discovery through the wilderness, I am able to connect the pieces of the puzzle to see the vision of wholeness of my God-given blueprint taking shape from all of the experiences, past and present. That Inn had been a place of despair for many who were not able to make it through the program, because they did not have eyes to see or ears to hear the plan the Lord had, to prosper and not to harm them. Some were not ready to heal and transform through the transitions and phases of the program that lacked direct connection to Christ. Some simply did not make it through the program because they were sabotaged by mean spirited people doing ungodly things and lying. It is unfortunate that as programs transform and transition through tumultuous times, Jesus Christ and the word of God have been removed. Some dwellers go from shelter to shelter looking for wholeness and healing, but without the Healer they are in constant search and constant wandering. Once God has been removed or never invited into a program or dwelling, those struggling with tormenting spirits stay on edge and push others to the edge also. If Jesus is not invited into a shelter, darkness will run rampant as spirits of darkness enter in with each new unbelieving resident.

Some Inn-dwellers are also brought to importunity, and seek out encounters with God. They learned to fervently pray and converse with Him in desperate need of answers for the questions that keep them awake at night, especially when disturbed by roommates and their tormenting witchcraft and dark spirits. Community living was very trying and really tests your walk in Christ: the way, the truth and the life. That was the most trying time of my life due to the number of people and daily changes. The house rules change daily, hourly and moment by moment depending on who you are speaking to at that moment. I realized many of the staff had issues as well, and if they had missed a few pay checks, they too could end up as residents. I could see and feel the stress and frustration of both staff and residents. The difference is, the staff members could go home, away from the drama, traumas and frustrations of Inn-dwelling. Someone's bright idea was to bring in new roommates without letting the current room occupants know a new stranger would be occupying the room with them. So, it felt like small shocks and traumas inflicted daily, increasing that feeling of having no control or choice in matters that affect you nor the time to process it. There was great concern due to the weak vetting process of those seeking refuge from the nut house or the big house. That, along with concerns regarding the backgrounds of others with drug, criminal and highly dysfunctional lives, which brought great fear to current residents coming from functional sheltered lives.

I discovered I was okay being cordial to lesbians and gender fluid people until one became my new roommate. I had to become compassionate to share this living space with peace. I realized had a more comfortable experience with the lesbian as my roommate than with the professed Christian woman as my first roommate. At one point during that year long stay, I was in that room with 2 lesbians who could not stand one another, so I tried to help by being the peacemaker for the 2 of them until the new one left after a couple of weeks. There were even a few one-night guests that did not remain in the room for various reasons. I found I was disgusted by the 3rd roommate, who was loaded with demonic spirits. She was the filthiest person, nosey, a thief, and socially inept. I believe my prayers moved several of them out like the one-night guests and those disrupting my peace until good roommates showed up in the room.

Community living was a trial by fire experience that tests one's ability and determination to persevere through the program. It took great faith to stay in the fire in the Inn, I had to remember that fire refines, so I had to stay in it to become transformed. I learned to be more compassionate to roommates with opposite backgrounds, habits, lifestyles and schedules as we lived in a small space together. I found it was very transforming, due to pressure and sometimes literally temperature changes in the room. It was also trial by fire for those staff members and counselors who worked with those dwelling in the Inn. Divine connections and divine open doors occurred with the staff and residents for all to learn lessons needed for each one's unique journey and development into a whole well-being. I believe nothing prepares or equips one for ministry and service as efficiently as first walking the walk of those you are predestined to be divinely connected to for service. I felt surrounded by the enemy, hard pressed on all sides by some of those who were supposed to help me. God can and will cause our enemy to bless us as we press forward into Him. As we remember we are in this world but not of this world, and we go through our daily tasks, pressing into Jesus, our stumbling blocks become our stepping stones, transforming us into the fiery stones we were predestined to become.

Importunity prepares the way for miracles as we speak the word of God and prophetic words into the atmosphere with urgency, persistency and fervency. Written petitions also prepare the way for miracles as we place these at the feet of

God. Petitions are supplications or pleadings for mercy, grace and favor. Jesus takes our supplications before Abba Father and our importune prayers bombard Heavenly realms, filling golden bowls to become incense from our sacrificial prayer, praise and worship as in the book of Revelation. Importunity increases our persistency and changes our character as we walk in faith, believing that what we speak will manifest for us. It's a challenge to balance importunity with humility and a contrite heart, being fully dependent on the faithfulness and goodness of God, yet coming boldly before His throne to speak our desires. Intercessors pray prayers of importunity, and Jesus and the Holy Spirit are our intercessors, praying importune prayers for us before the Father, and moving Heaven and Earth for us. I immersed myself in books on Miracles in this season. My hope and faith increased with each story or testimony of Miracles as I read the books, submerging my mind and heart in miracles. As deep calls to deep, some books appeared in my dreams or beaconed to me from the public library or book store shelves. I believe miracles happen daily; we just need to awaken to see and hear the extraordinary in the ordinary.

Jesus is the Author and finisher of our stories as he walks and writes with us, each word, sentence, chapter and book for each stage or season of our lives. As we ask, manna falls from Heaven; as we seek miracles occur, and as we knock, Inn doors are opened to prepare and equip us. Restoration manifests for us and those walking with us as fellow dwellers in Jesus Christ.

~Awake O you sleeper, arise!~

I found myself at what felt like another full circle moment in my season at the Inn, which confirmed that all things and events are connected and nothing is wasted. My prayer room season is now being used in various ways, as I have led several of those in my new community to this place of peace and discipleship. I have found that there are many distractions and hindrances in a homeless shelter that make it very difficult to focus on rebuilding one's life. There are constant changes, different personalities, negative energy, dark spirits, and other various issues. Sometimes it felt like a giant chess game with pawns moving from room to room by a master player seeking to capture kings and queens. It was a struggle to remain at peace with constant surprises such as room raids for contraband, drug and alcohol tests and the residents moved without warning, immediately thrown out back into the streets or evicted within days. The program was originally developed as a Christian program to help the homeless rebuild their lives, but many leave before accomplishing that goal due to all of the hindrances and darkness. Some are too fragile to handle the constant shifts, changes, surprises, and sabotage. Inn-dwellers are given no warning that a new stranger will be sharing their space. It was truly humbling to walk into your room and be surprised by a stranger. We never knew the background, lifestyle, issues, or the mental or emotional state of a new roommate until we are forced to get to know one another. In the midst of trying to heal, reset, rebuild and restore one's life, we were learning the rules, phases and processes of the program, while maneuvering through land mines of people's issues and triggers.

Many trigger one another without even realizing it, causing drama daily. I sometimes wondered how the staff continued to come back to work daily after very difficult drama-filled days, then I realized it is easier for them because it is not their life, they do not dwell in the Inn 24/7. They can go home to a place of safety and security. After a while it was obvious which staff members were there to help and which were there because they enjoyed lording over the down and out. No program or place is perfect because man is fallible especially if Jesus Christ is not the center of their lives, the focus of the place or program. In the Inn I found a few flames and some flickers of light in a sea of darkness; some puppets of Satan used to distract and hinder the progress of those called to big missions for God. Breakthrough to manifestation is tough even in the best circumstances: in peaceful environments with lots of alone time to excavate and evaluate one's past, present and future. The Inn experience was not for the weak or faint at heart. It was an emotional battlefield; mind fields of buttons being pushed, triggers pulled, and daily explosions that hinder and delay breakthrough. Some leave the Inn battle worn and in worse shape than when they arrived. There are some who are ready and willing to endure the pressures, and staggering blows as they utilize the program to accomplish their goals to reset, rebuild and restore, or create a whole new life for themselves and their loved ones. If an Inn-dweller is stuck in the clutches of pride, shame and embarrassment, they have not surrendered to humility, which is the key to freedom.

There was freedom in walking in faith and trusting there would be manna provided for tomorrow. Faith was knowing you do not have to hoard and save today's manna for tomorrow. Faith was also being obedient with the manna God provides to us. Manna was whatever we had need of: identity, peace, joy, love, provision and even protection. Some days the Inn felt like a den of lions and I could only imagine how Daniel felt as he awaited his miracle from God. There are many lions at the Inn, stalking for prey to devour, destroy, delay and distract with fear, confusion and disruption of destinies. The Inn should have been a place of restoration, but lions, large and small, are prowling about looking for prey to claw, bite, roar at or devour. This frightens others into running swiftly in the opposite direction, delaying their breakthrough and manifestation of restoration.

It was imperative that we seek God for our manna, directions and guidance at crucial times and junctures along our journey to renewal. We must seek God to recognize our opportunities and to know when to connect to and release others. The frightened prey in this pit of despair try to connect to those of us who appear strong, but if they are not walking or climbing in the right direction, they become a hindrance to us who are moving forward and upward at a different pace. I found that many of the Inn-dwellers are tortured by spirits of fear, rejection, abandonment and bitterness. Many have been frightened since childhood and are constantly living in fight, flight or freeze mode. These emotions go up, down and around like a roller coaster. Covid greatly increased the fear level of those already frightened by normal life. Many Inn-dwellers have raised themselves, and did not have functional families or role models to learn common daily skills for living a normal lifestyle. These Inns are plagued by the spirit of Leviathan, with conflict, confusion and gossip, fears that affects some greatly, due to ignorance, a lack of positive thoughts, and a lack of faith. Due to so many suffering from mental illness or emotional instability, there is constant drama in the natural and spiritual worlds. The enemy kept raising up its ugly head in the Inn with constant attacks and changes. The ones who were trying to do better seem to get evicted quicker than those just stuck and existing. Those trying to walk with Jesus who are new Christians, struggle greatly, and if they straddle the fence, they experience more chaos, causing many to go back to their old ways and foul living.

My year in the Inn was like watching a movie. It has had death, drama, thrills, sex, abuse, gossip, lies, and all the ingredients of a Hollywood best-selling film. There were characters from every walk of life playing new roles daily. Some knew they were in character, playing games created by the directors, and some were oblivious to what was going on around them. Some found themselves on lockdown, imprisoned by the ever-changing Covid quarantine craziness as rules changed at will by the puppet masters and those abusing power. I saw the shelter and surrounding property under a dome of gloom so thick like a dark snow globe without any cleansing snow or joy. A few who saw their doom about to unfold, entering lockdown with one of the unhealthy Inn-dwellers, escaped in time to avoid this outcome. Characters seem to come and go daily, like a movie set with its constantly changing story lines and new directions. There were minor stories playing out, connected to the big story. There were hidden agendas, and the director covering up events. Puppet Masters were pulling the strings, making others move and do the bidding of the director in order to sweep events under the invisible carpet lying under the invisible dome. It was mind-boggling to wonder how long and how many stories and narratives had been changed in order to keep the director and her puppet master minions in power. This was the darkest place I had dwelled, but I knew that the darkest dark brings out the brightest light. I felt like I needed combat boots to continue to live there, and I definitely needed to spend time in the Courts of Heaven to find strategies for manifestation of my restoration to be free from that very dark place. Sometimes it takes darkness to see the light like never before and seeing the bad to help us recognize the good.

Manna seasons are a time of trusting that God provides enough for us. We are to get what we need for today; our daily bread. Manna seasons help us break away from our past "how it used to be" mentality because manna is here and now connecting us to the present moment. Manna is also provided only in the wilderness seasons. In the Promised Land you get more than enough after being prepared and equipped, trusting as well as becoming willing and obedient to the leading of the Holy Spirit and Angelic instructions.

We have to recognize our manna our opportunities and apply importunity to make sure we one, recognize it and two speak and claim it and three give thanks for our manna remembering His awesome goodness and faithfulness in that season. God provided the Israelites manna in the morning seen as dew or frost on the ground so they had to recognize it as their answer to their prayers because it was in a form, they were not familiar with and likewise we must recognize our manna during our wilderness season. Just like the Israelites asked for meat and God sent quail, we must be mindful not to focus on the fare; manna or quail of our own past Egypt but be grateful for the new fare. In our wilderness season God gives us favor, like in Isaiah 55, to buy with no money. In our wilderness season we must claim every part of Psalm 23 because The Lord's table is prepared for us in the presence of our enemy with our daily bread; our manna laid out, beautifully arrayed for our benefit.

At the Lord's table we must express thanksgiving, gratitude, praise and worship. As we express gratitude it greatly changes and quickly shifts our attitude, bringing about a contrite heart ready to believe. Speak-then-receive as miracles and promises are laid out as a blueprint for us. "For as he thinketh in his heart so is he." Proverbs 23:7 The Key to walking in miracles is to believe with all our hearts that miracles can and will happen for us daily, as well as gratitude for the manna, which is also the Fruit of the Spirit. The key to walking in miracles is walking in the Gifts of the Holy Spirit and being grateful for the small and big moves of God. It is imperative that we are truly grateful for our journeys through our wilderness seasons. It is there that we are prepared and equipped the most, through the trials and testing along our journey. It is the wilderness that changes our mindset in each moment we express gratitude. In the dark seasons we learn to trust God and we learn to be obedient when it is toughest to follow some of God's instructions. These instructions and messages that come from God in various forms lead us to wellness emotionally, mentally, physically, spiritually and financially. As we come out of the wilderness stripped bare for others to see us authentically, we are able to clearly see divine connections that led us to our extraordinary well selves enabling us to help lead others along their pathways to their predestined manna, miracles and well-being too.

~Extraordinary New Day~

"You live life forward but you understand life backwards."

~Joyce Meyer

I praise You, for I am awesomely, wonderfully made!
Wonderful are Your works—
and my soul knows that very well. Psalms 139:14(TLV)

As I look back over the events that unfolded over the past decade or two in black and white, I am in awe of all that God has done for me and others. My life events and those of others revealed points of connection that weave a masterful design, reminding me of all of the angelic partnerships that brought divine connections to bless those involved in miraculous ways. I found that these divine points of connection allowed me to see, as a reflection in a mirror, patterns and cycles of traumas that produced emotional toxicity, black roots in my mind, physical pain and dis-ease, spiritual unrest and financial issues. I also saw these patterns and cycles in others divinely connected to me, and I found that experiencing all the traumas, cycles, processes, and miracles make us who we are destined to be according to God's plan before we ever arrived here on Earth.

During my awakening process, truly seeing God as everything that I needed and wanted in order to live a purposeful, passionate and productive life, I started asking questions of myself and others. As I got better at asking the right questions, I was led to the right answers; the ones I needed to unveil mysteries that I desperately wanted to understand about myself, others and the world. I was intrigued with people and the human experience through hardships to triumphant victories. I have always loved hearing stories of victory, and testimonies of unstoppable and unbeatable people with unfathomable odds against them. I feel so blessed to have been connected to so many women who were unstoppable and unbeatable. It was a pleasure to hear their stories and to watch each other's stories unfold. Once I found my root traumas, I prayed to seek guidance for what I needed to do, using the word of God to uproot everything caused by those original hurts. Divine connections taught and led me to eliminate emotional toxins, uproot black roots that produced black fruit in my mind, to speak to physical issues, to war in the spirit realm, and end my financial issues and call forth the promises of God to manifest in my life.

I matured into the knowing of how to walk as a joint heir as well as the bride of Jesus Christ. I learned to behave as a mature child of God, seeking wisdom, knowledge, understanding and how to give Godly counsel on how to live the word of God. The more intrigued I became, the more I sought the Lord and the more revelation I received through the scriptures, my visions and my dreams. I learned to walk in faith, speaking the word of God with boldness and confidence as I applied His word to my daily life. The more I spoke aloud the word of God, the more peace I felt emotionally. The Word brought alignment to my mind and heart, resolving not only the issues and problems in my life, but also the discomfort and pain of my body. The Word also told me who I was called to be spiritually, and it showed me the abundance of God's grace in my life.

It was a blessing and privilege for me to witness many people remove masks, both naturally and spiritually, to make peace with their true selves. It was also a privilege to help others find their root traumas as I searched for my own root traumas and triggers, like the words eviction and termination, that began certain cycles and downward spirals. I did the work needed for restoration, then I would guide others in the hard work that it takes to stop spiraling downward, hopefully before hitting rock bottom. It was a difficult process to stop the negative thoughts, words and behaviors that added to the misbehaviors of my body. Each time I would murmur and complain, or speak negative words, I felt pain in different areas of my body as these emotions took up residency physically. I was re-enforcing more of what I did not want in various areas of my life or worlds. I had learned to recognize my own negative recordings playing in my head, and I unknowingly repeated them over and over as I was triggered by various things, such as being evicted or terminated from a job. The rejections and moves, as well as the job terminations, were used to strip me and break me. But each move to a different residence or job brought divine connections to people, places and things needed to help in my transformation. My divine connections prepared, equipped, and trained me to also recognize the recordings, triggers, stripping and breaking of others, and to assist them as the Holy Spirit led. I would sometimes bluntly stop them from repeating negative words or declarations to stop a downward spiral, producing more bad toxins, roots and fruit, and vicious cycles of issues in all areas of their lives. As I reflect on the years through the cycles and circles of my life thus far, it looks like a massive roller coaster with various ups, downs, twists, turns and scary loops with stops along the way, some short and some long, due to derailments or obstacles, caused by traumas and triggers.

I felt like I had several full-circle moments as I sat in the Motel in my hometown after having moved away four years ago. As I sat praying and awaiting instructions from God, I was reminded of my first week of homelessness years ago when I sent my sons to their dad's house and I went to a Motel for a week to figure out my next step. I was blessed by a lady from my church who paid for that week at an Extended Stay Motel years ago. I was also blessed by several prayer warriors who sent money to one of my phone apps, covering my first week at the last motel stay before I moved to the shelter. God was showing me then and now that He is my provider as He orchestrates blessings coming to me.

As I sit reflecting and writing, I meditate on the story of Job. Like him, most of what I had had been lost, stolen or destroyed. It seems odd, but I find that I am filled with joy and gratitude to be at this point in my journey and at this full-circle moment writing at the end of the shelter program. I am not who I was years ago, and I am very grateful for all that I have learned and my relationship established with God. I spent that first week years ago petrified, filled with negativity, crying my eyes out because I felt so alone and clueless. I had no idea how to travel through this new territory. The long journey made me strong and I have gained peace beyond understanding because I know God is with me and He filled me with joy, no matter what was before me. God is my hope and I have seen Him move in miraculous ways for me, from that first week until this week, and He will continue to lead me into my amazing future. I was also filled with joy to be back in our hometown near my sons. I am grateful for the unique experience to have lived in that motel that was divinely paid for by prayer warriors, most of whom I do not even know. I am also grateful for my time at the shelter. Even though it was the most difficult time of my life, as I received blessings along my journey it was like God was winking at me as I gained knowledge that I never would have gained other than from these experiences. I am expecting God to move miraculously as I speak all of the prophetic words that have been given to me over years from week one until now. I sit in awe of God, awaiting my magnificent triumphant restoration or renewed life. Like Job, receiving a double portion. I am certain that it is time for payback, recompense and justice, because the enemy has been caught and judged. The Word of God says once a thief is caught, he has to payback with interest, and I know it will come forth. I trust that all of God's promises and prophetic words will manifest for me. The Word also says that we can request that the enemy's store houses and trophy rooms are to be plundered for us. I will use those spoils, my recompense, with interest, to build the businesses and the ministry blueprint that God gave to me while on this journey. It has been a long hard journey that I travelled, at times with Abba, Jesus and Holy Spirit as my only companions, especially when others were not able to understand what I was doing or why. Most of the time along my journey I could not explain, so I knew it was best for me to keep the other voices out of my ears while awaiting instructions and clarity for transitions from God and His prophets who confirmed His instructions to me. It is difficult travelling on the narrow pathways in some seasons, because sometimes I found myself at points on that pathway with few or no human companions in my presence. During those seemingly alone times, the only voice in my ears was that of God. If I chose to embrace my alone time with Him, knowing that he neither slumbers nor sleeps, and promises never to leave me, then I had peace beyond all understanding.

I am in awe as I wrote some of these chapters, but God showed me how to put them together in this book because originally, I wrote 21 chapters over the past decades. As one book it would have been a daunting task, so I was instructed by God then confirmed through some of His messengers to pull it apart, then rebuild it as a series. As I wrote some of this conclusion, or new beginning, as I prefer to call it, I was in awe of how much God loves me. I relished in the beauty of the Rocky Mountains in Colorado at a women's retreat, given to me as a birthday gift. It was my prayer that God would give me instructions on how to end this book while praising, praying and pressing into Jesus with over 200 other women on this retreat in the majestic mountains. I am in awe of the Rocky Mountains, with the Aspen trees turning vibrant fiery hues. I love most the bright yellow hue that the aspens wear for a mere few weeks. They speak of joy to me, which was part of the subject matter for this retreat, as the speakers each taught from the book of Philippians. Paul speaks of joy at least 16 times in various words through the book of Philippians. As I previously stated, the Lord had told me on various occasions that "Joy is my weapon". I was so filled with joy as I basked in this amazing scenery, seeing the majesty of the work of His hands as He sculpted the Rockies, so beautifully arrayed with clusters of vibrant Aspens on soaring peaks. I am so grateful for each respite like this retreat from the Inn, and from the stripping process to be refreshed and to gain new perspective and instructions.

As I sat journaling during my retreat in the Rocky Mountains, gazing at the works of His hands, both nature and His children, I was amazed seeing the magnificent beauty in the brokenness of each woman who spoke about the symbolism of the Amazing Aspens, and sharing their testimonies and God given messages. I found that our brokenness brings usefulness for God's glory. God used each speaker to help me reflect on parts of this book, beginning with the first speaker who spoke on "Coming Along Side" which reminded me of the Titus women in my life and the one He wants me to become. The next speaker spoke on "Unity" in the correlation between the Aspen trees and the body of Christ. Our stories, testimonies and scars show evidence of our brokenness bringing openness to help the body of Christ arise and shine non-apologetically. Then another spoke on being created uniquely for our calling. I had been asking God how to end this book, this part of my testimony, and that of the women who crossed my path and shared their testimonies. They taught me so many lessons through losses, and I gained blessings through new choices and new mercies. Every end brings with it a new beginning, and God is the author and finisher of our stories. He is the Alpha and Omega, the beginning and the end. Knowing of Jesus is why this story began and truly knowing Him intimately is how this story will finish. There is healing in the name and blood of Jesus, and this book, these pages, chapters, sentences and words all point to Him. As we seek to connect to Him and remain connected to Him, we can lead others to connect to Him also. We must grow our relationships with Him for our roots to go deep and produce more fruit for personal nourishment and sustainability for our journeys.

New cycles of healing, development and growth equip us to help others and serve others in our ministry; our service to those connected to us. Our ministry is birthed out of our greatest challenges. That Rocky Mountain retreat blessed me greatly as an opportunity to fellowship with like-minded women and to be refreshed after spending months with so many at the lowest points of their lives in the Inn. God brought me to a beautiful place of refreshment to marvel at the work of His hands. I was greatly blessed to relax and reflect on my journey in a Hot Spring as I look at the magnificent Rocky Mountains. Then the last woman spoke on the word "Think" and it was a message from God for me to finish this book as I started it. This retreat is manna from Heaven, filled with messages and confirmations needed to help me complete the assignments and tasks necessary to prepare and equip me to leave the past and spring forward into the new. I was blessed to be in a retreat center drenched in praise and prayer from all of the Christian groups who found respite within the Rockies, in this town and facility. I believe in Miracles because I chose to see them daily in my life and in the lives of those who are divinely connected to me, or those who crossed my path even for brief moments.

That was the most restorative and revelatory weekend, with over 200 women on the mountain tops all praising, praying and pressing in to the Lord as one body and one voice. The Women's Ministry decoration theme was the Aspens; as transformation of the Aspens took place outside, transformation of the women took place inside. Just like the Aspens grow best in threes, like a three-strand cord not easily broken, we grow best with like-minded others. These glorious trees teach us so much about how we should be as trees of life. Many times, trees have been used in the word of God to symbolize man, so we should learn from nature. Audacious Aspens quiver, quake, and whisper messages in the wind, and if we have eyes to see and ears to hear we are greatly blessed by them. Beautiful groves of Aspen draw crowds to them due to their brilliant Autumn Hues. Aspens are pioneers who quickly take up residency in sites disturbed by fire, in bare soil or on gravelly and sandy slopes. Aspens were created to quickly bring an area that appears to be destroyed and devastated back to life by producing 50 to 100 thousand sucklings from root sprouts, or seeds from their collective root system to quickly populate an acre of land that was desolate. The word of God says even the rocks will cry out, so surely the Audacious Aspens cry out daily to God as their leaves quiver, quake and whisper in the wind. They also speak to each other through their root system. God put intelligence in everything He created, including trees, and we have much to learn from nature as the body of Christ. Aspens symbolize connectivity, victory, and rebirth. As we connect and share our collective stories and testimonies of miracles, we help bring back to life the dreams of others. The sharing of our stories helps others to know they are not alone in the midst of their awakening to the presence of God. We help others as midwives to birth and rebirth God-given dreams, businesses and ministries to walk in their victories too.

At this point in my journey, I realize that the value I had placed on things no longer mattered, and that I have nothing left to lose, as I have been stripped completely bare, except everything of true value, gaining the things money cannot buy. I have nowhere to go but up from where I am in the natural. I have been brought low in the natural, but it provided the energy to fuel my ascension higher, spiritually focusing intently on God's voice, the only voice in my ears most of the time in this season. I learned to live with my Maker as my husband. God is my everything: my provider, protector and partner in everything. My identity and purpose come from and through my connection to Him. I learned that I can count on and have expectations of God only. I cannot and should not have expectations of any man or woman, because humans are fallible creatures who will fall short of our expectations at some point. My roles are now based on who He calls me to be at any given moment, and I am willing and obedient to follow His leading or commands because I love Jesus. It has taken me a long time to understand true unconditional love and trust, which is only found with and through Jesus. On my own I am not capable of loving and being filled with compassion to show grace and mercy to others. I need God to walk everything out with me. As others forsake or abandon us and harm us with their deeds, we must turn to the one who will never forsake or abandon us. His deeds are done with unfailing love for us. He also helps us to forgive others, knowing they will fall short sometimes.

I am able to walk as a Proverbs 31 woman with Jesus as my husband, my maker, my friend and so much more. As I fell in love with Jesus my transformation got easier because I saw him with new eyes, filled with love and awe. My heart was healed as I fell in love with Him, I experienced an amazing love that I have never known before now. I also felt the love of Abba Father as prophets were sent to tell me that he says, "You are special to me, you are loved just as you are and that you are the apple of my eye.". My heart was connected to the heart of God through encounters with my triune God over the years. The Holy Spirit has been a wonderful friend and comforter to me like no other. I am encouraged to seek to be a better friend to others. I am learning in each extraordinary new day to receive love from God, then love and show lovingkindness to others. I do my best to be a virtuous woman as described in Proverbs 31, knowing He values me and chooses to use my voice, my hands, and my feet as I yield to Him daily. I am grateful for new mercies every morning because only with and through God am I able to aspire to become the virtuous woman I am destined to be: new and evolved each extraordinary new day.

"Her husband is famous and admired by all, sitting as the venerable judge of his people. Even her works of righteousness she does for the benefit of her enemies. Bold power and glorious majesty are wrapped around her as she laughs with joy over the latter days. Her teachings are filled with wisdom and kindness as loving instruction pours from her lips." Proverbs 31:23-26 TPT

Over the years, I have learned the difference between wants and needs as I went from owning 10 houses to being homeless with 10 bags. As He uses me, I know my purpose here on Earth is to be a voice and a messenger amongst many in the throat of the body of Christ by sharing messages from Abba Father's heart. I am here for more than my goals, my accomplishments and living my version of the American Dream. I have spent the past decade and a half learning to be and do what The Word of God says. I know that I have not yet arrived at full maturity or am not fully bloomed yet. My daily goal is to seek to be willing and obedient and to walk in the perfect will and timing of God according to his plan for me.

I know that I have a lot of work ahead of me to serve humanity with my voice, my hands and my feet as well as the rest of this body in a way that is unique to me. But I now know, I am wonderfully made for such a time and season. I know an abundance of provisions are needed to put into action the blueprint that God gave to me and I know he will provide all that is needed for His mission and glory. This book is about my journey from owning 10 houses to being homeless with 10 bags, and the journeys of women who crossed my path and those whose paths ran parallel to mine in various seasons. This book is also about how I got here, to my full circle Job moment of restoration and manifestation, transformed and renewed, but still a masterpiece in progress. All that I have learned over the past years is needed for my kingdom purposes and destiny to be fulfilled. I am so excited, as well as thankful, that the promises of God as prophesied to me are manifesting as I speak and believe them to be established. I exercise my childlike walk-on-water faith, trusting The Word of God that He put in my heart, as my dreams, goals and affirmations become my true reality daily. The Word of God shows me that I don't have to settle for less than what was prophesied, because I can have what the Word of God says I can have, I can do what the word says and I can be everything the word says according to the books in Heaven already written about me, my purposes and my destiny. This book is simply a guide to lead each of us, including myself, on a closer walk with Abba, Jesus and Holy Spirit. It will also guide us through each new day along our pathways created especially for each of us to lead us to our purposes, passion and pinnacles of our lives.

The most powerful thing for moving forward is to decide when enough is enough, then turn to Jesus Christ when you know you are not who, what and where you are destined to be! As I would write, read, re-write and re-read this book over the years, it became a guide for me as well. Since it encompassed many years of ups, downs, twists and turns, I have endured numerous derailments, and this book guided me back on track. We must make the choice to follow the leading of Holy Spirit, then take that guidance, put it into action to change the cycles, hardships, and downward spirals to use His power to provide the energy for our momentum upward and onward into victory. We must decide whose word we are going to receive and believe; that of the one who created us or that of those well-meaning people who do not know the plans that God has for us or that of the adversary, who is trying to harm us. We must decide to use our God-given free will and our God-given gifts to be who we were destined to be from the beginning of time. We become the choices we make as we choose to follow the word of God through our human experiences. When we choose not to follow the word of God, we get out of alignment with God and find ourselves struggling, laboring and toiling in every area of life. As we choose to connect and remain connected to Abba Father, Jesus and Holy Spirit, we are guided through our journey of life, the crooked places are made straight, and that which was meant to harm us is used to train, equip and mold us to properly handle our missions. As we submit and surrender to being trained for our missions it shows Jesus that it is our heart's desire to be in alignment with the perfect will of the Father.

I found that nothing is wasted, even the things or skills that we think are obsolete. God will direct us in how to repurpose, reposition and regenerate everything to serve us and others in our missions. There were dreams and goals that I sometimes thought may not manifest after so many years of hoping and praying while my faith developed and grew with each answered prayer. I was deceived to think these dreams and petitions were denied as things appeared to get worse, not better, especially while in the shelter with none of my vision boards in sight. I continued to press through the program with fervent prayer, spending as much time as possible in the prayer room as my safe haven of peace. I had to hold on to hope and continue to speak with faith that my dreams were just simply delayed, awaiting the perfect timing to come forth. I am so grateful for how I was trained in how to repurpose, how to repeat the words of God to reignite the fire of faith for those dreams to manifest in the right season. I learned it was imperative for manifestation that I was repositioned in the right place, at the right time, with the right people and with the right attitude of gratitude for each season of my life. My regeneration and restoration were needed so that I could make the right choices, take the appropriate actions, and handle the responsibility of being a good steward. I truly believed that learning to be at peace without the stuff, the trappings of the American Dream, would give me confidence to be a great steward of the blessings he promised me. I realized His dreams were my dreams because they were in my heart as we became one. I found that as I walked with Jesus as my husband, I longed to please Him. But I learned His love for me was not based on my earning it, His love was freely given to me. I learned I was deeply loved at my best and at my worst by Jesus, Holy Spirit and Abba Father. I also learned that as the bride of Jesus, I did not have to handle the responsibility of my mission alone, for God partners with me the moment I yield to Him. Handling the responsibility of my mission and dreams also means having the strength to be led by God's instructions because the mission and dreams are ours to handle jointly. I gained the strength to use wisdom to say no to the requests of people, when necessary, as directed by Holy Spirit. After many years of saying yes when I knew I should have said no to some people, I learned a lot about being disobedient to God. Spirits that caused a false sense of obligation to people, many of whom were clueless about the meaning of reciprocity and reciprocal relationships, as well as being obedient to the leading and guiding of Holy Spirit. I learned that "NO" is a full sentence, and to say it non-apologetically and mean it by sticking to it, because saying no is showing lovingkindness, especially when I know that I heard God regarding the matter at hand. I do not want to get in the way and knowingly hinder the growth of others by being a crutch or forming codependent ungodly soul ties.

As I look back over the years, I understand why some prayers were answered a bit differently from what I expected or what I requested; for example, I prayed for a debt-free car but instead of a silver SUV that I asked for, which would have cost more than I could afford to insure and maintain in a tough season, I was blessed with a small grey compact hatchback car. In God's infinite wisdom and grace, He touched hearts to provide what I needed as a blessing without the car causing a hardship for me. I know of several women who were blessed with vehicles they struggled to insure and maintain due to the cost associated with that make and model. As I look back over the years, my faith grew from walking on the surface of the water faith to walking on the air faith, inviting me to step off of the cliffs I could see onto what I cannot see with complete trust in the Lord. I developed a knowing that I am always safe in His mighty right hand. I learned who I was as the wife of Jesus my provider, protector and role model, who guided me in my search for significance that I found in simply yielding to His will daily. I was awakened by knowing the plans He has for me as I walk in my God-given roles along the highways and byways connecting with well women also in search of significance and keys to unlock our worlds. I realized how strong and courageous I was by baring it all to breakthrough, and removing the facades that I allowed to cover and hide my true essence and worth, which did not come from owning, or shall we say having, 10 houses with mortgages. I was greatly blessed to see and understand the grace of connections as I connected to God heart-to-heart and connected hand-to-hand with those along my path. I excavated and found my brokenness was true beauty hidden beneath ashes now serving as fertilizer, helping me bloom in great splendor and confidence in his garden. I was made aware as my true self and essence was exposed, and as I embraced and loved the new ever-changing me along my journey, I felt more empowered and confident in my purposes. I gained clearer vision during unprecedented times, traveling light with my 10 bags when forced by circumstances to look at everything through new eyes of faith, seeing the ordinary as extraordinary, as manna and miracles occurred daily for me and others. I am accepting the endings of old things and joyfully anticipating new beginnings that I see springing forth with each spectacular day. God's unconditional, unfailing, unending love is very real to me now, and I feel more safety and depth in being His beloved with each new day.

"And you did not receive the spirit of religious duty, leading you back into fear of never being good enough. But you have received the "spirit of full acceptance," enfolding you into the family of God. And you will never feel orphaned, for as he rises up within us, our spirits join him in saying the words of tender affection, "Beloved Father!" For the Holy Spirit makes God's fatherhood real to us as he whispers into our innermost being, "You are God's beloved child!" Romans 8:15-16 TPT

Romans 8:15 sets us free from bondage and fear of the performance standards of others as we know we are Abba Father's beloved child, which sets us free from an old mindset of measurements and lack, because we are children of the King of Kings. We must walk in Authority and Confidence knowing our dominion to bring down everything needed from Heaven to Earth as portals or Jacob's ladders for ascension and descension to do the work of our father here on Earth. We are carriers of glory and the river of God which flows in and through us as we exercise our faith when we know our Father as Abba Father. All things are possible with and through Jesus Christ, who is everything that we have need of. As we speak the word of God, all things are healed and all our prayers are answered for ourselves and others. These pages bare the connections and revelation I needed to make to walk in well-being along my journey from having 10 houses to having very few possessions. We walk in well-being emotionally, mentally, physically, spiritually and financially when we surrender to a willing and obedient walk, trusting God no matter how the path looks or feels. Through trust we are wholly connected in intimate relation to Abba Father, Jesus and the Holy Spirit. As we are being guided through each extraordinary new day, we become more like Jesus as a mature son of God in each joy-filled day. The Joy of the Redeemed, His beloved, is to walk in The Way, The Truth and The Life of Jesus through the stages of nakedness, being stripped bare before the eyes of God, free from hindrances, wholly connected, and completely well. It is my prayer that you have found your nakedness, and brokenness has made you more beautiful and valuable in the Kingdom of God. This has occurred because of every step taken and every tear shed through your wilderness journeys: walking in faith, hope and love. I pray that this series will assist you as a transformational guide for a smooth transition to our God-given destiny. I also pray that you, His Beloved, will see that you are blessed beyond your wildest dreams as you are stripped Bare to see manifested promises and the divine Connections that created; Extraordinary You to bare it all in prayer!

"Happy is she who believed that the Lord would fulfill the promises he made to her." Luke 1:45 (CEB)

~ *End Notes* ~

1. Leaf, Caroline. *Switch On My Brain*
      Ada: Baker Publishing Group, 2015
2. Thurman, Chris. *The Lies We Believe*
      Nashville: Thomas Nelson, 1989
3. Miller, Sandra. *Balancing Blessings and Obtaining Order*
      Maryland: ByB e-Publishers, 2009
4. Eggerichs, Emerson. *Love & Respect*
      Nashville: Thomas Nelson, 2004

~ *About The Author* ~

Jonquil Guidry is a mother, writer, speaker, entrepreneur, Certified Life Coach and Real Estate Broker. She is a creative, intuitive, and self-motivated individual, who relishes the opportunity to help change lives. Jonquil has held positions ranging from receptionist to management to business owner. Her professional knowledge, skills and expertise were gained from many years in the Multilevel Marketing, Direct Sales, Retail, Wholesale, Education, Insurance, Banking, Stock and Annuity Brokerage, Mortgage Brokerage, Real Estate Brokerage and Real Estate Investing Industries. She spent years being very active in organizing mastermind and meet-up groups as well as being a member of various community organizations.

Jonquil grew up in a military family, where she travelled and experienced diverse cultures; which enables her to bridge the gap between herself and others quickly to establish a connection or common bond. She has gained knowledge, skills, and expertise from her personal experiences. As she transitioned through divorce and health issues, she went from riches to rags. Consequently, she learned how to recover, rebrand, rebuild, and recreate streams of income to transform her life emotionally, mentally, physically, spiritually, and financially. As a result of Jonquil's Journey from owning 10 houses to becoming homeless, it is her heart's desire to share her journey to encourage other women like herself. In her transition from having more than enough resources to none, she had to learn how to deal with the traumas associated with losing the lifestyle, she had become accustomed to living. She also desires to use her insight gained to help other women in similar situations recover quicker than she recovered. Jonquil started her journey of hardships as a single mom with school aged sons under her roof then she became an empty nester in one day and she hopes to prevent others from enduring this heart wrenching experience. She has spent many years learning and utilizing holistic healing modalities out of necessity to create wellness and balance in her life. Her passion is assisting women in transforming their lives by sharing her journey and helping them navigate their struggles to grow spiritually, eat well, seek peace, and rebuild wealth. Jonquil has 3 grown sons and they all reside near Dallas, Texas.

Connect with Jonquil online:

www.jonquilconnections.com and
www.10housesto10bags.com

YouTube: www.youtube.com/@10housesto10bags

Instagram: jonquilconnections

Facebook: Jonquil Guidry

TikTok: @JonquilG

Address:

550 N Central Expwy #159

McKinney, TX 75070